- Most people experiencing PTSD have another disorder as well, such as depression, severe anxiety, or substance abuse, which can sometimes mask the diagnosis of PTSD.

- About one quarter of those who experience a severe trauma will develop PTSD and at least 40 percent of the population will experience a trauma that puts them at significant risk.

- When friends and loved ones develop stress-related symptoms, they are known as co-victims and they too may require professional intervention and treatment.

- PTSD damages our ability to use emotions to make sense of the world. People with PTSD tend to lose their ability to experience even the "good" emotions.

- Studies have proven a variety of medical conditions can be related to stress and trauma, including headaches, rashes, backaches, stomach problems, and susceptibility to colds and flu, diabetes, hypertension, and even heart conditions.

LEARN THE CRUCIAL FACTS PLUS THE LATEST INFORMATION ON NEW TREATMENTS, ALTERNATIVE THERAPIES, SCIENTIFIC BREAKTHROUGHS, AND MUCH MORE IN . . .

WHY AM I STILL SO AFRAID?

The Dell Guides for Mental Health

Why Am I Still So Afraid?

Understanding
Post-Traumatic Stress Disorder

John W. Barnhill, M.D.
and
R. K. Rosen

A Dell Mental Health Guide
Series Editor: Roger Granet, M.D.

A DELL BOOK

Published by
Dell Publishing
a division of
Random House, Inc.
1540 Broadway
New York, New York 10036

Dell books may be purchased for business or promotional use or for special sales. For information please write to: Special Markets Department, Random House, Inc., 1540 Broadway, New York, NY 10036.

Dell® is a registered trademark of Random House, Inc., and the colophon is a trademark of Random House, Inc.

ISBN: 0-440-23464-6

Designed by Donna Sinisgalli

Printed in the United States of America

Published simultaneously in Canada

August 1999

10 9 8 7 6 5 4 3 2 1

OPM

This book is dedicated to:
My family —JWB
My parents, Hannah and David Liknaitzky —RKR

Acknowledgments

Special thanks to our literary agent, Judith Rivin, for her editing skills and continued support on this project.

Contents

Foreword

Over twenty million Americans will get post-traumatic stress disorder. It is an equal opportunity illness, striking down people of every race, creed, and national origin. It affects people from all walks of life and in every region of every country on the planet. While some of us may be particularly prone to getting the disorder, any of us is potentially vulnerable. Also known as PTSD, post-traumatic stress disorder is a common problem with uncommonly serious effects. While treatable, PTSD often inflicts its damage on people who aren't even aware that they have the disorder.

The first goal of this book is to make the diagnosis of PTSD clear to you. We will begin by describing the official psychiatric diagnostic criteria, but in order to help the diagnosis come alive, we will also provide numerous examples of people with PTSD. Our second goal is to help you or your loved one recover from the disorder. To do this, we will discuss treatment options that range from individual psychotherapy to group therapy to medication. In addition, to enrich your understanding of both the diagnosis and treatment, we will elaborate the current understanding of what causes PTSD in the first place.

It may be useful to know that PTSD has always been with us. Under other names, it has been described in the works of Plato, Shakespeare, and Freud. Since the beginning of recorded history, some of the sharpest observers of human nature have noticed that people sometimes develop a particular behavior pattern after a severe trauma. This constellation of behaviors, feelings, and thoughts can be confusing and is one of the reasons that it was difficult to come up with a consensus on what PTSD really is.

While the symptoms of PTSD can be confusing, there is a clear set of guidelines for its diagnosis. Within these guidelines, however, there are many, many possible variations. It is these variations that tend to confuse everyone, whether they are clinicians or the general public.

One way to understand PTSD is to look at the words that make up the diagnosis. *Post-traumatic* stress disorder must occur *after a trauma*. When referring to PTSD, the trauma must be outside the range of normal human experience and must feel overwhelming. Rape, child abuse, natural disasters, and combat are probably the most common examples of such trauma, but there are many others. Trauma does not refer to a mild argument at work or disappointments with a spouse. When we are talking about PTSD, in other words, the trauma must be severe. It does not, however, have to be especially rare. Many people with PTSD have been traumatized many times, sometimes over a period of months or years. In fact, PTSD tends to occur in people who have been repeatedly traumatized, though it can occur after just one terrible, overwhelming experience. Problems may occur immediately after the traumatic event, though there can be a lag between the event and PTSD symptoms. Most notably in cases of child abuse, PTSD can develop months, years, and even decades after the traumatic event. In PTSD that develops years after the event, we tend to find serious memory gaps involving the trauma; the person with PTSD may have blocked all memory of the event and be able to retrieve only murky recollections. At times, the recollections aren't even words but vague physical feelings. The first condition of PTSD—that it occur after a trauma—may seem clear at first glance, but the reality is that it may be difficult to document even the serious trauma. This is the first possible confusion in PTSD, but it's not the last.

The second half of "PTSD" is *stress disorder*. This is not the same thing as stress. After a serious trauma, everyone gets stressed. In PTSD an overwhelming trauma imprints itself so intensely that people develop a *stress disorder* that must include a specific, characteristic constellation of symptoms. For example, everyone with PTSD develops signs of being overly aroused. A person with PTSD might complain of feeling irritable or being easily startled or having trouble falling asleep, for example, but these would all be considered signs of being overly aroused. A second core symptom of PTSD is "reexperiencing" the traumatic event. Nightmares and flashbacks are examples of reexperiencing. The final core symptom of PTSD is the effort to avoid anything related to the event, which might mean avoiding thoughts, people, feelings, or memories of the trauma. Related to avoidance is "numbness," which might mean feeling detached from other people, not taking pleasure in the activities of life, or not being able to anticipate having a future. Everyone with PTSD has symptoms from each of these three categories: overarousal, reexperiencing, and avoidance/numbing. We will elaborate on these symptoms in greater detail in the course of the book and give lots of examples to make them clear.

It may be very helpful just to realize that your or your loved one's condition has a name—PTSD—and that it can be diagnosed and treated. Understanding the nature of PTSD is often the first step in a person's recovery, especially since most of the people who have the disorder don't know what name to put on their confusing array of problems.

As an additional complicating factor, people with

PTSD often have other psychological problems. For example, the anxiety that is part of PTSD often causes people to abuse drugs and alcohol. The addiction may be obvious and destructive, and the PTSD may get ignored and be left untreated. Similarly, many people with PTSD are depressed. Depression is relatively easy to diagnose, and so the PTSD may not be properly evaluated. This can lead to a depression treatment that isn't effective for PTSD. The possibilites are many, but the importance of a correct diagnosis is clear. Without this clarity, the treatment is likely to be ineffective.

Once it has taken hold, post-traumatic stress disorder can be difficult to treat, even if it is properly diagnosed. Some of you may know full well that you have PTSD, and yet you have struggled for years to overcome the disorder. Others of you may have just been traumatized and are trying to prevent the development of full-fledged PTSD. In the chapters on treatment, we will cover both of these examples, and everything in between.

While there are lots of possible treatments for PTSD, we believe that there are two central aspects to recovery. First, it's important to develop an ability to relax. This may seem obvious, but people with PTSD often find it nearly imposssible to get comfortable. In fact, if you are relaxed while reading this book, you probably don't have PTSD. The hallmarks of PTSD—arousal, reexperiencing, and avoidance/numbing—are all anxiety symptoms. In people with PTSD these symptoms can be haunting and can make life feel unlivable. An essential goal of therapy then, is to develop a sense of ease and relaxation. There are many ways to develop such feelings and we describe a range of possibilities. You might want to try some or all of them.

A second aspect of treatment is reexposure. This reexposure could be to physical reminders of the trauma, but we are mainly talking about exposing your mind to thoughts and feelings that bring forth associations or memories of the traumatic event. By chewing over the painful memories and feelings, your mind can gradually make some sense of the trauma. In so doing, the experience becomes less overwhelming and can become integrated into your general experience of life. Some of you may be helped by understanding the brain physiology of PTSD, since it fits in neatly with this point of view, and we describe current theories in some detail. At the same time, an interest in biology is certainly not a requirement for understanding the message of this book.

You might have noticed that the two core aspects of treatment—relaxation and exposure—are at odds with each other. If you have PTSD, you are probably well aware that it feels impossible to relax when you are reminded of the trauma. In fact, avoidance of such exposure is one of the cardinal symptoms of PTSD. In the course of this book, we will discuss this built-in problem and describe ways to deal with it. We will also describe how a variety of other people have successfully dealt with this problem.

The anxiety associated with PTSD can be disabling in a variety of ways. In order to treat themselves, people with PTSD may become addicted to drugs or alcohol. To limit their fear, they may avoid new experiences and, in so doing, gradually retreat into a shell, losing themselves in loneliness. PTSD can cause haunting nightmares and "daymares." It can cause eternal jumpiness, irritability, and poor concentration. Simply put, PTSD can sap life of its pleasure and meaning.

If PTSD were easy to diagnose and easy to treat, you'd have already figured it out by now. If PTSD were a self-limited problem, like the common cold or seasonal allergies, your PTSD would just go away by itself. But PTSD is different. It tends to stick around, building up its power, gradually taking over more and more areas of your life. The underlying goal of this book is to help you turn this cycle around, to help wear down and digest a disorder that may feel like it has taken over your mind. Recovery from PTSD is possible, but it does require that you acknowledge and approach the problem. In this book we try to teach you how to approach and control PTSD, a journey of self-discovery that may be the most rewarding effort you ever make. Woven through the book is the recognition that comfort is vital, that recovery from PTSD requires an ability to relax and enjoy the small and large pleasures of life. Good luck with your journey, and in the meantime, try to be kind to yourself.

—*John W. Barnhill, M.D.*

Cornell University Medical College
New York, New York
April, 1999

Chapter 1

WHAT IS POST-TRAUMATIC STRESS DISORDER?

Post-traumatic stress disorder (PTSD) is the name for an illness that has been present since the beginning of recorded history. At the same time, its symptoms have been complex and confusing and have frustrated the countless people who have suffered from it as well as all those who have tried to help the afflicted. The goal of this book is to help you get a handle on just what this diagnosis means and to offer some suggestions on ways it can be treated.

What makes it so complicated?

Post-traumatic stress disorder is a relatively recent term for a constellation of symptoms that can be hard to organize neatly. PTSD must begin after a trauma, but the trauma might be a train wreck that happened last month or sexual abuse that occurred in early childhood. At the time of occurrence, the trauma must have immediately caused intense fear, helplessness, or horror, but these feelings might not even be remembered by the time the person seeks treatment; and, in children, the immediate response might be disorganized or agitated behavior rather than a feeling. Although the trauma must be "reexperienced," the recollections may take place in several ways. They might be in the form of clear memories, nightmares, physical feelings, reenactments, or distress when exposed to something that reminds them of the traumatic event (like a war veteran hearing the backfire of a car). In addition to reexperiencing the event in some fashion, people with PTSD must also avoid reminders of the trauma and numb their general responsiveness, and they must present symptoms of increased arousal. Each of these terms and the general categories of "avoidance" and "arousal" are simplified expressions that reflect wide-ranging symptoms in human beings.

As can be seen, there are lots of ways that this disorder can present itself. In addition, most people experiencing PTSD have another disorder as well, such as depression, severe anxiety, or substance abuse, which can sometimes mask the diagnosis of PTSD.

I think I might have PTSD, but I don't really understand what you're saying. If it's so complicated, how am I going to recognize it?

The goal of this book is to allow everyone to understand the basic concepts of the disorder and to consider treatment options.

Consider the following scenarios:

- Jim is a Vietnam vet. He has difficulty falling asleep. When he does doze off, he is tormented by nightmares that are sometimes so vivid that he shakes and pushes his wife, terrified that he is back in Vietnam and that she is the enemy. He has complained about sleep problems for years, but his family doctor has quit giving him sleeping pills, saying that sleeping pills and alcohol don't mix. Jim knows this is true, but he also believes that beer helps him in several ways. According to Jim, a few cans of beer stop him from exploding at all the daily frustrations of life, help him get to sleep, and help squash the nightmares. People say he should just get over it, that it's been thirty years since he was in the war, but he is just feeling worse and worse. And now his wife says she can't stand the physical abuse at night (he has been known to assault her in his sleep, mistaking her for the enemy hidden in the jungles of Vietnam) and his irritability all day. His relatives think he's an alcoholic, and he is afraid that his wife may want a divorce. Jim wants to change, but he doesn't know where to begin.

• While Lilly was walking home from work one night, she was wrestled into the woods and raped. She felt like a wreck afterwards, unable to sleep or relax. It's been six months, but she keeps thinking of the man's face. She never walks home anymore, but takes the bus, even though it's slow and out of her way. In fact, she gets very anxious at the thought of going anywhere near the woods. She quit her softball team, because all the games were held at a park, and the park reminded her of the woods. Her whole body shakes when she sees a stranger who reminds her of the man who raped her. She now has great difficulty going out on dates or being alone with men. She obsesses about what she should have done to prevent the rape.

• Fred, a paramedic in a small town, was called to the scene of a terrible traffic accident during a blizzard. A school bus carrying nine children had skidded off a cliff and crashed into the rocks below. The children and the driver were killed. Fred felt his whole body go numb at the scene of the accident, but he was able to help remove the bodies from the wreckage. While he seemed to be doing okay immediately after the accident, images of the school bus preoccupied him for months. His whole body seemed to alternate between being numb and being sensitive to any little stress. He decided to quit working as a paramedic. This helped a little, but almost anything reminded him of the accident: children, buses, snow, the cliffs. He convinced his wife to move to Florida, to get a fresh start. This helped, but he knows he's still not the same.

- Beverly started seeing a therapist last year because of persistent depression. She knew she should have seen the therapist sooner, but she'd never liked talking about herself. She'd finally relented because another of her boyfriends was complaining that she was uptight, spacey, and moody. As she and the therapist started talking about her difficulties with intimacy, a vague, nauseating sensation came over her, which then stuck with her for days. She'd never really enjoyed foreplay, but now she began to feel creepy whenever her boyfriend even touched her. She started to have terrifying dreams in which a giant rat was eating her. After a few weeks of these dreams and creepy feelings, Beverly had just about decided to stop therapy. She'd been depressed before, but now she was worse. Suddenly she began to have images of her first stepfather doing sexual things to her when she was a young child. The images seemed very clear, and there were lots of them, but they also seemed unreal, as if they'd happened to someone else. Could she possibly have forgotten something so major? That stepfather had disappeared when she was five. She'd never given him a second thought. How could he have done this? She began to feel dirty and contaminated and more depressed. She had lots of thoughts of hurting herself and a few, dim feelings of intense rage. She certainly wanted nothing to do with her boyfriend. And she wasn't so sure she wanted to continue with her therapy.

In many ways, Jim, Lilly, Fred, and Beverly may have little in common, yet each is suffering from PTSD.

I've started hearing and reading a lot about PTSD. Is this condition something new?

While doctors have been studying and treating victims of trauma for centuries, the diagnosis of PTSD wasn't included in the psychiatric diagnostic manual until 1980. Prior to that time, people with PTSD symptoms were diagnosed and treated in a variety of ways; often their situation simply went unrecognized.

How did PTSD get recognized in 1980?

Apparently the efforts of three separate groups forced a review of the diagnosis. Vietnam veterans, women, and therapists began to challenge the status quo.

How did these groups help to change the diagnosis?

The Vietnam War exacted a huge toll on American soldiers, even ones who sustained no physical injuries. During their periods of service, these young men and women often experienced immense psychological and physical trauma. For our purposes such trauma might have been caused by working at a field hospital, having many friends killed, or actively participating in killings. These events can overwhelm anyone. When experienced by young people who find themselves in a strange land, with easy access to mind-numbing drugs and alcohol, no strong conviction in the meaning of the war, and an enormous lack of support from home, the feeling of being overwhelmed is intensified. As we will discuss later, each of these variables increases the risk of PTSD, and many of the men and women who returned from Vietnam did develop cases of PTSD. On their return, however, a diagnosis of PTSD didn't exist. Instead, their symptoms were seen as a combination of depression, anxiety, and substance abuse. Treatment was attempted with limited success.

At the same time, the women's movement was gaining strength on a variety of fronts. Earlier women's rights activists had pushed for greater political rights. During the 1970s women worked to gain greater control over their bodies. In regard to PTSD, this was expressed as a determination to recognize the widespread physical and sexual abuse that women suffered in this country. They looked for treatment programs that specifically addressed their needs. They didn't find very much.

Vietnam veterans and abused women seemed to have little in common. They did, however, share a common problem: post-traumatic stress disorder. While continuing to go to individual therapists or, more often, suffering in silence, they began to insist on a recognition of their problems. This grass-roots movement was critical to the acceptance of PTSD as a discrete disorder. At the same time, there was a movement within psychiatry and psychology to evolve crisper, more focused treatments for people suffering from a variety of problems, including PTSD. And with the advent of new experimental techniques, mental health professionals learned a great deal about the psychology and the biology of PTSD. The coincidence in timing of the efforts of these three distinct groups helped to open up the field and make treatments more available, more specific, and more effective.

There must have been people with PTSD before 1980. What happened to them?

War and tragedy have caused suffering since the beginning of time. All observers have noticed that. PTSD is not, however, simple suffering. It is a set of symptoms that occurs after a trauma, and these symptoms can be pretty confusing. Nevertheless, a constellation of unusual reactions to trauma has been noticed for centuries. Herodotus, an ancient Greek historian, described a soldier who was so overwhelmed by the death of a friend that he lost his vision. Similarly, Homer wrote of the overwhelming rage and impulsivity of two soldiers (Achilles and Agamemnon) after the trauma of battle. Shakespeare's Hamlet falls apart after the murder of his father. He demonstrates the cardinal symptoms of PTSD: arousal, avoidance, and reexperiencing. His faith in his family and himself shattered, Hamlet feels enraged, distrustful, depressed, and suicidal. He can't make up his mind about anything and has terrible nightmares. Even though the official diagnosis wouldn't be made for four hundred years, Shakespeare understood PTSD.

How has PTSD been understood during the last one hundred years?

The recent history of PTSD is, to some extent, the recent history of psychiatry. The rest of this book will describe various aspects of PTSD, but all the dilemmas of the diagnosis have been around since Sigmund Freud began writing one hundred years ago. Love him or hate him, Freud's ideas remain critical to the understanding of PTSD. Freud believed that psychiatric disorders could be caused by psychological trauma. Most of his contemporaries, however, believed mental illness was caused by biological or neurological defects and that treatment was hopeless. Freud was more optimistic and spent the next forty years trying out different treatments. He believed that much suffering was caused by

traumatic memories that could be forgotten and held in
the unconscious, where they caused anxiety. The only
way to get rid of these unconscious memories was to
talk about them in a free way. This led to the development of psychoanalysis as a treatment method. In his
earliest writings Freud tended to see the victim as being
relatively passive. As he developed his theories, he
came to believe that people are more active, that our
perceptions and our character play an important role in
how we interpret the events of our lives. Treatment
evolved, therefore, from simply talking about our
memories to talking about our perceptions, fantasies,
and defenses. All current treatments for PTSD are
based on these ideas: A psychological trauma has occurred and our minds block the memory of the trauma.
This strategy provides some relief but causes great suffering. Treatments are necessary to bring out the memories safely so that we can process and extinguish
them.

If Freud's ideas are accurate, why do people criticize him all the time?

His ideas were, and are, controversial. In regard to sexual abuse, he decided that some of his patients had
misremembered events from their childhood and that
they were claiming child abuse when none had been
committed. He continued to believe that real trauma
caused problems (he called it traumatic neurosis), but
he shifted his focus to the role of unconscious motivation in mental illness. His observation that some people
misremember their childhoods is true—modern therapists recognize that memory plays tricks on us all—
but his shift in focus may have led to the underestima-
tion of real sexual abuse in our society. In addition, his
writings emphasize the role we play in our own problems, that we are unconsciously responsible for our ac-

tions and for much of what happens to us. This may or may not be true, but it does lend support to a blame-the-victim mentality. This conflict between victimhood and personal responsibility remains a lively issue in terms of PTSD, as it does with many issues in our culture. Our attitude within this book is that the development of PTSD doesn't mean the victim should be blamed. At the same time, people with PTSD have the ability to get better, with help. There is some conflict in that assessment: if you can get better, then isn't it partly your fault that you're still having problems? This is the sort of dilemma that we all struggle with and that people with PTSD often struggle with most of all. This book should help you come to terms with such dilemmas.

What did Freud have to say about war veterans?

After twenty years away from the subject, Freud renewed his interest in actual trauma during the First World War. Many soldiers were coming home incapacitated, and Freud and his fellow psychoanalysts began to treat them. Freud noted that people with what we would now call PTSD had a characteristic pattern of alternating between intrusive and avoidant symptoms. He thought that these back-and-forth efforts were an attempt to master the trauma. He also noticed that many such people tended to have nightmares, which he also felt were part of a compulsion to gain control over an uncontrollable event. One psychoanalyst coined the term "physioneuroses" as a way to demonstrate that PTSD combined psychological and biological issues. Yet another psychiatrist coined the term "shell shock" to describe this condition.

If "shell shock" was becoming well known, what did psychiatrists do to prevent it?

By the time of the Second World War a screening process was designed to eliminate the enlistment of men who might not possess adequate psychological strength. Psychological trauma continued to take a huge toll during this war, despite the perceived importance of the effort and the support of friends and family back home. It was becoming increasingly clear that PTSD could happen to anybody if the stress was severe enough. By the time of the Vietnam War it was decided that soldiers would serve no more than thirteen months at a time, in the hopes of reducing psychological problems. This strategy didn't work to prevent PTSD either. Many Vietnam veterans returned to the United States with what would become known as PTSD.

Was all the focus on combat soldiers?

Much of it was, though other doctors studied the enormous psychological trauma inflicted on concentration camp survivors and prisoners of war. These people had even higher rates of "shell shock" than did soldiers. Given the devastating experiences that they went through, this isn't surprising. Over the next few decades, therapists treated survivors of the traumas of this war.

At about this point, the Vietnam War and the women's rights movement began to develop strength, and the PTSD diagnosis was born.

What was PTSD officially called before 1980?

Prior to 1980 the disorder was seen to be part of a depressive neurosis or anxiety neurosis, which are terms that aren't specific enough to describe the condition adequately.

Why is a clear definition of PTSD so important?

A clear definition of PTSD is important because it gives a name to a group of vague and elusive symptoms. When a condition has a name, it becomes tangible and is easier to recognize and to understand. In addition, it helps victims realize that the way they are feeling and behaving is due to a massive trauma rather than a sign of weakness. A clear definition also facilitates an accurate diagnosis, which paves the way to an effective treatment. For example, the treatment of depression or anxiety differs from the treatment of PTSD. If PTSD is the cause of your depression, but you are treated only for depression (for example, with medication), you may not recover from the PTSD. If the underlying cause of your problem has not been properly diagnosed, it cannot be properly addressed. Medication may help with your feelings, but it is possible that you will continue to experience problems related to unresolved trauma in other areas of your life.

How common is PTSD?

A study done by the U.S. government in 1995 estimated that 8 percent of the U.S. population will have PTSD at some point in their lives. This would be equal to about twenty million people. About one quarter of those who experience a severe trauma will develop PTSD, though this percentage varies quite a lot, depending on the type of trauma. At least 40 percent of the population will experience a trauma that puts them at significant risk.

What kinds of trauma tend to cause PTSD?

Initial reports showed that most men with PTSD had been in combat and that most women with PTSD had been victims of rape and sexual molestation. In recent years a flurry of studies have shown PTSD to be more widespread. One study found that among a group of

300 drug-abusing teenagers in Boston, 45 percent of the girls qualified for a PTSD diagnosis, as did 24 percent of the boys. Another study showed that one quarter of people who had sustained mild head injuries in car accidents developed PTSD six months after their accidents. Children of Holocaust survivors have a high risk, as do police officers, firefighters, emergency medical technicians, victims of violent crime, and prostitutes. Natural disasters often cause PTSD.

Which traumas are more likely to cause PTSD?

Three variables of trauma intensity seem to predict who is likely to get PTSD: severity, frequency, and duration. We will talk more about these later, but you should keep in mind the common-sense idea that PTSD is more likely if the trauma is more terrible, if it lasts a long time, and if it repeats itself.

Are these statistics likely to increase in the future?

That depends on a variety of factors. As victims become more comfortable speaking up about their experiences, crime statistics may increase. We have already seen a dramatic increase in the reporting of domestic violence and sexual abuse, and this could lead to a greater reporting of PTSD. The increasing dislocation of families and the rising incidence of poverty have led to the loss of traditional support systems; this could continue to increase the incidence of PTSD. At the same time, our society seems to have developed a greater sensitivity to the trauma of poverty, violence, war, and natural disasters. As a result of these changes, we may be better able to recognize and treat the victims of PTSD. The future of this disorder is very much in our hands.

How do I go about getting help?

That's the purpose of this book. For one hundred years PTSD has been under investigation, and major strides have been made in the area of treatment. Securing the right treatment, however, is not always easy and will involve some preparatory work on the part of either the victim or those trying to secure help for him or her. This means doing some research to find the most suitable therapist or treatment program in your immediate area. We will deal with this in greater depth in Chapter 6, "Finding Help." As far as treatment is concerned, each case is different and there is no single miracle cure. Together with your therapist, you will need to come up with a series of techniques that suit your individual symptoms and personality.

Is it possible to have PTSD and yet be unaware that you have been exposed to trauma?

Yes. Sometimes people develop the symptoms of PTSD but don't know why. It could be that you are suffering from full or partial amnesia as a result of your experience. Perhaps you were too young to remember the event or perhaps your mind actively chose to forget what happened, in an attempt to shield off pain. Sometimes traumatic experiences go with the territory of a particular job. In the course of duty, firefighters, police officers, and ambulance paramedics routinely come face-to-face with life-and-death situations and thus may not be aware that symptoms such as anger, depression, insomnia, or substance abuse may be related to their job.

Are women more prone to getting PTSD than men, or vice versa?

No, the development of PTSD is not related to your gender. If you are exposed to a traumatic event, you run the risk of developing PTSD. Victims of rape and domestic abuse tend to be women, and combat veterans have almost always been men. It has been shown, however, that men who have been raped or physically abused often develop PTSD, as do women who experience combat.

What effect does age have on the development of PTSD?

Children are particularly vulnerable to severe trauma because they haven't yet developed strong defenses against the trials and tribulations of the world. At the same time, children are often quite resilient as long as they are provided active and appropriate support by trusted figures in their lives. Old age can also be a risk factor for PTSD. Older people are often victims of violence in our modern society, and they are often left with declining resources, declining health, and distant relatives.

Are other groups at risk?

Any vulnerable group is at risk. For example, poor single mothers tend to lack the support of family and society and are more likely to be victimized by boyfriends and thieves. People who abuse alcohol and drugs are also at risk. Not only do these drugs lead people into dangerous situations (and therefore trauma), they limit the ability to feel, and numbness is a major risk factor for PTSD.

How can I tell if I have PTSD?

We will list the official requirements for a diagnosis of PTSD in a later chapter. At this point you might want to look at the questionnaire below, which was developed so that the layperson could get a feel for the disorder. The questionnaire doesn't substitute for a professional evaluation, but it might help you find out whether you need to pursue more professional help. Be aware that some of the questions may cause you to experience intense feelings and memories. If this occurs and you find it overwhelming, it would be best to discontinue working through this assessment on your own. Move on to the next section of the book or discuss your feelings with your doctor.

What are the requirements for the diagnosis?

There are four requirements. First, you must have been traumatized. Second, you must have three types of symptoms that relate to the trauma. These three symptoms are: reexperiencing the trauma, avoidance of reminders of the trauma, and hyperarousal. We'll go through each of the four and use the questionnaire designed by Aphrodite Matsakis.*

You say that the first requirement for the diagnosis is a history of trauma. What qualifies as a trauma?

Many situations in life are scary and stressful, but not all such events are traumatic, according to the official definition. The following questions will help you determine whether or not you have been traumatized. If you answer yes to any of these questions, you have experienced trauma.

- Have you ever experienced a natural disaster—an earthquake, tornado, fire, flood, or landslide?
- Have you ever experienced a community- or work-

* Reprinted from *Post-Traumatic Stress Disorder: A Complete Treatment Guide,* by Aphrodite Matsakis (Oakland, Calif.: New Harbinger Publications, 1994), by permission of the author and publisher.

related disaster such as an explosion, chemical spill, or an exposure to radiation?

- Have you ever lived in a concentration or refugee camp?
- Have you ever been tortured?
- Have you ever been sexually or physically assaulted?
- Were you ever physically maltreated as a child with excessive beatings?
- Were your parent's/caretaker's disciplinary measures sadistic?
- Have you ever witnessed the death, torture, rape, or beating of another person?
- Have you ever seen someone die or be badly injured in an accident?
- Has anyone in your family or a close friend been murdered?
- As a child, did you ever witness the beating, rape, murder, torture, or a suicide of a parent, caretaker, or friend?
- Have you ever been kidnapped, abducted, raped, robbed, or mugged?
- Have you ever been badly injured in an accident or as a result of a criminal episode?
- Have you ever been involved in a war—either as a civilian, soldier, medic, or member of a support team?
- Have you ever been involved in any situation where you felt at the time that you or a family member would be badly harmed or killed?
- Have you ever been a member of a medical or firefighting team, a police force, or a rescue squad where one of the following conditions occurred:

–danger to your safety and life

–witnessing death and injury

–making life-and-death decisions

–high-stress working conditions (long hours, unsafe conditions) .

So, everyone who has experienced a trauma qualifies for a PTSD diagnosis?

Even if you have experienced trauma (that is, you answered yes to any of the above), you do not meet the criteria for PTSD, according to the American Psychiatric Association's *Diagnostic and Statistical Manual of Mental Disorder,* Fourth Edition (or DSM-IV), unless you have responded to the situation with intense feelings of helplessness, fear, or horror. You must also meet the three criteria that we already mentioned: reexperiencing the trauma, demonstrating avoidance behaviors, and showing signs of hyperarousal.

You said that the first symptom of PTSD is reexperiencing the trauma. What does that mean?

The traumatic event has ended. You should feel safe. Yet you continue to relive the trauma in some way. This is reexperiencing. The following list of questions will help to determine whether or not you are reexperiencing the traumatic event. In order to meet the DSM-IV criteria, you must answer yes to at least one of the following questions:

• Do you have persistent, recurring, intrusive thoughts about the event? Do these thoughts or visions pop into your head even if you are trying hard not to think about them?

• Do you have nightmares that are about the event or are somehow related to the event? Do they either take place in the same location or cause you to feel the same feelings of helplessness, fear, and anger that you suffered during the original event?

• Do you ever feel like you are back in the event (flashbacks) or have visions or hear sounds pertaining to the event?

• Do you ever have strong emotional reactions (feelings of anger, fear, anxiety, etc.) close to the anniversary date of the trauma or around people or events that remind you of the original trauma?

• Do you ever have strong physical reactions (sweating, hyperventilation, dizziness, or pain) close to the anniversary date of the event or when you are exposed to events that remind you of the original trauma?

If you have not had any of the above experiences, you probably do not suffer from full-blown PTSD. However, you may still suffer some of the symptoms, which can and should be healed, so read on.

The second symptom you mentioned was avoidance. What does that mean?

In addition to reexperiencing, people with PTSD practice avoidance. In other words, they block feelings and avoid activities associated with the trauma. Be aware that these feelings or behaviors must have begun after being traumatized and not before. In addition, avoidance is often done outside of conscious awareness.

• Do you ever have periods when you feel numb or dead inside?

• Do you ever have periods when you are unable to have loving feelings?

- Are the feelings you do experience predominantly those of anger, hatred, or resentment?
- Do you feel alienated from other people?
- Are you no longer interested in activities that previously gave you pleasure?
- Do you feel a sense of doom, that you will die young or never be able to experience the normal rewards of living such as having a family, a career, etc.?
- Is it difficult for you to remember certain aspects of the traumatic event?

The final symptom you listed is hyperarousal. What does that mean?

People with PTSD show symptoms associated with increased arousal. These might be insomnia, irritability, or always being on the lookout for danger. Review the following list of questions to determine whether you are suffering from this characteristic symptom of PTSD. Remember, as with the criteria for avoidance behavior, these symptoms must have begun *after* the traumatic event occurred to be considered a symptom of PTSD. This is because most of the following symptoms can be associated with other physical and psychological conditions.

- Do you have difficulty falling asleep?
- Do you have trouble staying asleep or is your sleep disturbed in some way?
- Do you feel irritable or tense a lot of the time? Do these feelings cause you to act in irrational and antisocial ways?
- Do you have trouble concentrating?
- Are you overprotective (hypervigilant) about your safety and the safety of those you love?

- Do crowds make you anxious?
- Are you easily startled? Do you jump at loud or sudden noises or at noises that remind you of the trauma?

If you experience symptoms in all of the above three categories, then you most probably have PTSD.

Can PTSD be treated?

Yes, it can. No one need struggle with the painful, intrusive thoughts and the overwhelming feelings of alienation, fear, and low self-esteem that are caused by PTSD. With the right treatment many of these symptoms can be helped and maybe even eliminated.

I have some of the symptoms of PTSD—how do I know if I need treatment?

Severity of the condition differs from person to person. Some people may suffer the symptoms so mildly that treatment might not be necessary. Others may find that their lives are a disaster. If your symptoms do not interfere with normal life activities, then even though you may have suffered trauma, you probably do not have PTSD. On the other hand, if your symptoms do interfere with your ability to love, have intimate relationships, be productive, or participate in the activities that make life pleasurable, then you need to seek help. Many studies have shown that people with acute PTSD tend to become chronically ill without treatment.

What is the difference between acute stress disorder and PTSD?

Most of us suffer some symptoms of psychological distress during or immediately following a traumatic event. For example, we might feel anxious, helpless, detached, and angry. We might avoid anything associated with the trauma. We might have bad dreams or be afraid to leave the house. We might recognize that our life has been temporarily disrupted. If our problems have lasted less than one month following the trauma, then we would have an acute stress disorder.

Is there a way to prevent an acute stress disorder from becoming PTSD?

To reduce the likelihood of PTSD, you can do a variety of things. Get away from the traumatic experience and get safe. Make use of friends, family, and social supports. Talk about the trauma with trusted and/or knowledgeable people in a comfortable environment. Acute stress disorder usually resolves spontaneously. If symptoms last longer than a month, or if they appear months or years after the traumatic event, then this response is called PTSD.

How can this book help me?

This book is designed to help people with acute stress disorders or PTSD and to help people whose loved ones or friends have one of these disorders. Each chapter is composed of a series of questions and answers that address the most important issues related to PTSD. Further readings on PTSD are listed in the bibliography in the back of the book. You will also find a listing of organizations where you can secure help. Remember, you are not alone. Help is out there. There are ways to restore happiness and balance into your life.

References
Bryant, R. A., and A. G. Harvey. "Relationship Between Acute Stress Disorder and Post-Traumatic Stress Disorder Following Mild Traumatic Brain Injury." *American Journal of Psychiatry* 155:5, May 1998, pp. 625–628.

Classen, C., C. Koopman, R. Hales, et al. "Acute Stress Disorder as a Predictor of Post-Traumatic Stress Symptoms." *American Journal of Psychiatry* 155:5, May 1998. pp. 620–624.

Deykin, E. Y., and S. L. Buka. "Prevalence and Risk Factors for Post-Traumatic Stress Disorder Among Chemically Dependent Adolescents." *American Journal of Psychiatry* 154:6, June 1997, pp. 752–757.

Flannery, R. B. *PTSD: The Victim's Guide to Healing and Recovery.* New York: Crossroad Publishing, 1992.

Kessler, R. C., A. Sonnega, et al. "Post-Traumatic Stress Disorder in the National Comorbidity Survey." *Archives of General Psychiatry* 52, December 1995, pp. 1048–1060.

Krystal, H. ed. *Massive Psychic Trauma.* New York: International Universities Press, 1968.

McCarroll, J. E., C. S. Fullerton, et al. "Post-Traumatic Stress Symptoms Following Forensic Dental Identification: Mt. Carmel, Waco, Texas." *American Journal of Psychiatry* 153:6, June 1996, pp. 778–782.

Matsakis, A. *Post-Traumatic Stress Disorder: A Complete Treatment Guide.* Oakland, Calif.: New Harbinger Publications, 1994. (1–800–748–6273; www.newharbinger.com)

Trappler, B., and S. Friedman. "Post-Traumatic Stress Disorder in Survivors of the Brooklyn Bridge Shooting." *American Journal of Psychiatry* 153:5, May 1996, pp. 705.

Chapter 2

WHAT CONSTITUTES A TRAUMATIC EVENT?

What kind of trauma can cause post-traumatic stress disorder?

When we talk about PTSD, we are talking about an experience in which someone is faced with an event that is psychologically overwhelming. This event may be life threatening or may threaten the person's integrity as a human being. In addition to being seriously traumatic, the experience must elicit intense fear, helplessness, or horror. It may occur once, as in a rape, or may occur sporadically over a period of years, as in some cases of child abuse, or it may be a prolonged experience such as being a prisoner of war.

I lead a very stressful life. Will I develop PTSD?

Life is by nature stressful for most of us. But people do not develop PTSD from leading stressful lives. PTSD is only caused by being exposed to "true trauma."

What is the difference between stress and "true trauma"?

The word "traumatic" is often loosely used. We use it in everyday life to describe incidents that cause us to experience loss or to feel stress. We use it to describe a particularly difficult day, the breakup with a boyfriend or girlfriend, or the loss of a job. Although stressful, these events are not considered to be "true trauma." Truly traumatic events are so terrifying that the person experiencing the event is rendered absolutely powerless. According to the DSM-IV, a traumatic event is any situation that involves immense danger, one that is, or is perceived to be, life threatening. And it is an event over which we feel we have no control.

Traumatic events are often sudden, unexpected, and deemed "out of the ordinary" in that they are not what one would expect from day-to-day living. If, for example, you watch your elderly parent die after a long illness, the event, though stressful and sad, would not be considered traumatic, because it is not unusual for one's elderly parents to die from illness. If, however, you witness your mother being brutally beaten to death by an intruder, the event would be classified as traumatic, because being beaten to death is not a normal way for an elderly person to die.

What kinds of events are considered traumatic?

Traumatic events are those events which we perceive to be catastrophic and which overwhelm our ability to defend ourselves. They might involve death and injury or they might involve the destruction of something or someone we value. Some traumatic events are caused by nature, including floods, earthquakes, tornadoes, tidal waves, avalanches, and volcanic eruptions, and some are inflicted by other humans, as in combat, terrorism, kidnapping, torture, physical and sexual assault, violent crime, serious accidents, and bombings. Severe illness, anesthesia, surgery, or other hospital procedures can also cause traumatic reactions (especially in children).

Is it possible to develop PTSD if the traumatic event did not happen to me directly?

Yes. If you witness a traumatic event happening to someone else or even if you hear about something terrible happening to a loved one, you can develop the symptoms of PTSD. For example, suppose several members of your immediate family were killed in a horrendous plane crash on their way back from a two-week vacation in Miami. Although your life was not directly threatened, the magnitude of your loss could cause you to develop PTSD.

It is also possible to develop the symptoms of PTSD if you grow up with a trauma survivor and learn stress responses from them. For example, if your father, a war veteran, dives for cover every time he hears a clap of thunder or a car backfire, you might learn that diving for cover is the appropriate response to a loud noise. This is called transgenerational transmission. Similarly, a child might hear graphic details of an event that traumatized a parent and internalize the event to such a degree that he becomes traumatized and learns to react to particular stimuli as though he were exposed to the event himself. For example, a young girl may develop an aversion to men after hearing her mother talk about being raped. This is called secondary traumatization. Secondary traumatization and transgenerational transmission are common in severely traumatized families, such as Holocaust survivors.

Does the type of violence experienced affect one's response?

Yes. Violence against a person is generally felt to be worse than violence against property. For example, most people would be more traumatized by a robbery at gunpoint than by having an equivalent amount of property stolen during a burglary. The event would be even more traumatic if the robbery led to physical violence and you were severely beaten. The more brutal the violence, the greater the potential for developing PTSD.

In addition, it appears that people are better able to cope with natural disasters than they are with atrocities committed by other humans. It has been speculated that this may be because acts of nature are pretty much out of our control, while violence committed by other people shakes our sense of safety and trust. This brings up the important issue that the severity of trauma depends very much on our perceptions of the trauma rather than on an objective assessment of the damage or violence.

What factors determine the impact of the traumatic event?

Factors such as severity, frequency, and duration have great influence over the effect of a traumatic event.

How does severity affect the development of PTSD?

PTSD develops after a demoralizing and overwhelming event. The worse the trauma, the more likely it is that PTSD will develop. For example, studies show that PTSD developed in only 8 percent of soldiers who participated in the Desert Storm conflict, whereas it developed in at least 30 percent of Vietnam veterans and in 75 percent of survivors of concentration camps. In these cases, severity of trauma seems to vary based on fairly obvious levels of danger and powerlessness. Another important aspect of "severity" is the person's perspective on the trauma. For example, suppose two men lose their arms in accidents. One is a construction worker whose family depends on his daily work for their survival. The other is a business executive who rarely does physical activities. Both men will be traumatized by their accidents, but it is likely that the construction worker will be more severely traumatized.

What is meant by the "duration" of an event?

The longer an event or a series of events continues, the greater the impact may be. Events that have circumscribed time limits (like hurricanes) or events that occur for short periods of time (like muggings) are easier to resolve than events that continue for an extended period of time (many cases of domestic violence or incest). As the trauma wears on, coping skills are eroded, and it becomes increasingly difficult to think accurately about the situation. In particular, the development of a feeling of helplessness underlies the development of PTSD, and the longer the trauma drags on, the greater the likelihood of PTSD.

How does the frequency of trauma affect the development of PTSD?

The more frequent the trauma, the more likely it is that PTSD will develop. One study of Native Americans showed that the average person without PTSD had experienced only two traumatic events. The average person with PTSD had experienced twenty-three different traumatic events. The researchers found that people who had experienced more than ten traumatic events were eight times as likely to get PTSD than were people who'd experienced fewer than ten traumatic events. It doesn't seem to matter whether the traumatic events are the same or different; frequency of trauma is a major risk factor for PTSD.

Does experiencing the event with others as opposed to being alone affect the impact of the traumatic event?

Yes. Studies have shown that people suffering together provide each other with emotional support, companionship, and a sense of solidarity that make their individual burdens easier to bare. Groups of people "in the same boat" are able to pool their collective wisdom and problem-solving skills, which engenders positive action and group empowerment. This fact has led to the successful use of support groups for people who have been victimized.

Do cultural differences play a role in how different people experience trauma?

They can. Some cultures stress the value of maintaining close family relationships or strong religious convictions. These can give meaning to life, even in the face of great adversity. And in some cultures, expressions of thoughts and feelings are encouraged, while other cultures may view this as a sign of weakness. Being able to express how you think and feel is essential both to your recovery from PTSD and to its possible prevention, so being part of a culture where expressiveness is encouraged can be beneficial. Likewise, living within a culture that discourages such expression can impede your recovery from trauma.

Do different cultures view victims of trauma differently?

Yes. Some cultures promote the silent, private endurance of suffering, whereby individuals who have experienced trauma are encouraged to maintain a "stiff upper lip," to put the event behind them and to carry on as if nothing has happened, without involving others. There may be something to be said for being able to keep a stiff upper lip, but on the whole, a forced denial of suffering will do most people more harm than good.

On the other hand, some societies believe that a problem for an individual represents a problem for the whole group and thus collectively embrace a person who is suffering, because they believe that healing the individual will benefit the society as a whole. This practice is found among some of the more shamanistic cultures.

Does everyone who has been exposed to a traumatic event develop PTSD?

No. The percentage varies a lot, but generally speaking, about 25 percent of the people who experience a severe trauma go on to develop PTSD. On the other hand, almost everyone has some sort of stress reaction after experiencing a trauma.

Are some people more at risk for developing PTSD?

Well, yes and no. There are in fact a number of factors that can increase your risk of developing PTSD after being exposed to trauma, but it cannot be overemphasized that in spite of these possible risk factors, anyone exposed to sufficiently high levels of stress is at risk for developing PTSD.

What are some possible risk factors?

Studies have shown that a variety of factors may play a role in the development of PTSD. These include being traumatized as a child, having a genetic predisposition, having a history of abusing drugs and alcohol, and living without social supports. We'll discuss each of these in more detail, though we should also add that many people develop PTSD without clear risk factors.

I was sexually abused as a child. Does that make me more likely to develop PTSD as an adult?

While no risk factor determines everything, a past history of abuse does put you at increased risk. As children we all develop a lot of coping skills, and there is a normal trajectory of development that we all tend to follow. However, although children who have been abused may develop a whole host of strengths, they are often "stuck" in regard to some aspect of their development. An abused child often develops feelings of distrust which she tends not to outgrow without help. As an adult her feelings of distrust may lessen and she may grow into a wonderful wife and mother. But if she is confronted with a tremendously traumatic experience as an adult, such as a rape or natural disaster, her earlier problems with trust could intensify her reaction to what is already a horrible situation. She might then involuntarily give up certain strengths that she has developed over the years, and her earlier feelings of being abused, alone, and scared would be rekindled. These feelings would increase her risk of PTSD.

Am I more likely to get PTSD if the trauma was committed by someone that I know?

Yes. Betrayals by friends and family are generally much more damaging than assaults by strangers. For example, sexual or physical abuse inflicted by a parent or spouse is not only a violent criminal act, but also one that violates your basic sense of trust. Mothers, fathers, husbands, and wives should be protectors and caregivers, people we can depend on for nurturance and support. Our intimates are not supposed to be criminals, rapists, or tyrants. If loved ones torment us, the world becomes unsafe and unpredictable. People tend to defend against such trauma by disbelief and numbing, telling themselves that their loved one couldn't possibly be so bad. This is especially true in children, but we also see this psychological defense in battered spouses. These feelings of disbelief and numbness underlie the development of PTSD, especially when the trauma is a betrayal that would tend to cause rage and frustration.

My father was an alcoholic who became physically violent whenever he drank. Would coming from this kind of background put me at risk for developing PTSD?

Yes, very possibly. Alcoholic families are usually dysfunctional and therefore do not teach good coping skills. If you have not been taught the proper skills needed to cope with the ubiquitous stresses of life, you will probably be at a marked disadvantage if exposed to another serious trauma. In particular, families tend to deny the extent of the parent's alcoholism, and denial of reality is a risk factor for PTSD. In addition, some people who grow up in such chaotic environments have low self-esteem due to years of parental neglect. They may perceive themselves as unwanted and unloved. This can have serious consequences when trauma strikes, because low self-esteem can lead to heightened feelings of powerlessness and helplessness.

Would my age affect my chances of developing PTSD?

Yes. As previously discussed, age and life experience affect how we react to trauma. As we age, we tend to develop a stronger sense of ourselves and a greater ability to deal with pain, grief, and stress. Children, adolescents, and young adults are at risk because they have not yet developed the skills needed to cope with stress and also because they do not have the insights or the experience needed to put traumatic events into perspective. In addition, they have yet to develop actual control over practical aspects of their lives, so they generally lack the wherewithal and physical prowess to leave or control traumatic situations.

Is it possible to have a genetic predisposition to developing PTSD?

Yes. Some people, due to their particular biological/genetic makeup, become more aroused than others when exposed to stressful events. You may sweat more profusely than others, your heart may beat faster, and your body may release greater amounts of adrenaline in response to stress. In other words, some people have a naturally intense physical reaction to even mildly stressful events. Some people also remain in a chronic state of physical arousal for longer periods of time than others. If your body responds intensely to stress, or retains its aroused state after the stress has passed, your symptoms may be highly intensified when severe trauma strikes. You are probably more likely to develop PTSD if a serious trauma should strike.

How serious a risk factor is the cumulative stress of daily life?

A series of stressful events that occur in quick succession can wear on your resistance. If, for example, over a period of several months, you lose your job, lose your marriage, and lose your dog, you may be more vulnerable to PTSD. If you then get robbed at gunpoint, these cumulative stresses would increase the likelihood of PTSD.

I am a heavy drinker. Does this increase my chances of developing PTSD?

Any serious addiction definitely increases your risk of PTSD. Alcohol and drug abuse hurt your overall physical health, which would predispose you to PTSD. Even more importantly, mind-altering substances lead to poor judgment, impaired memory, and irrational behavior. These psychological changes lessen your ability to deal with trauma when it does occur, and they also make you more prone to being exposed to trauma in the first place. Finally, drugs and alcohol induce an altered state of consciousness, which is a specific cause of PTSD and a specific roadblock in the path to treatment.

Does a history of mental illness increase my risk of PTSD?

Yes. Any serious mental illness increases the risk of developing PTSD.

Would being forced to suffer the trauma alone, without the support of others, increase my chances of developing PTSD?

It seems that a person who is forced to suffer the trauma without the caring support of friends or family or without the support of society is more likely to go on to develop PTSD. Just knowing that someone out there cares is enough to help lessen the impact of the trauma. A prisoner of war may, for example, hold himself together during difficult times by remembering that he has a loving wife and family waiting for him at home.

As is well known, Vietnam veterans returned home to an antihero's welcome. In addition to having to deal with the atrocities they might have experienced, seen, or inflicted on others, these veterans often had to deal with these problems alone. Further, many veterans returned home with a drug and/or alcohol addiction. Many of them developed PTSD, a problem that a number of them are still dealing with thirty years later.

Victims of sexual abuse and rape have also had to go it alone. These are crimes that have historically been hidden and felt to be shameful. These victims' increasing visibility and political power have been important factors in the improved prospects for people with PTSD. Not only does such clout provide a greater measure of control, it also allows people with PTSD to develop sources of support and connection more openly.

If I fall into the high-risk category, will treatment be more difficult?

No. Being in the high-risk category only influences your chances of developing the condition. It doesn't generally affect the treatment. It's a bit like the flu. If you've been working long hours during the virus season, you may become run-down and more susceptible to catching a cold or flu. But flu is flu. Once you have it, treatment is much the same. And that generally holds true with PTSD as well. Regardless of the risk factors, much of the treatment is the same. As with the flu, however, you should pay attention to what might have contributed to the development of your PTSD in the first place. This might mean getting plenty of rest, not drinking, and reducing the overall stress of your life.

Can my environment affect my chances of developing PTSD?

Yes. Having access to a safe and protected environment allows freedom from repeated traumatic events. Having good community resources can mean the availability of shelters, self-help groups, and mental health services. Being part of a supportive society or family can provide invaluable financial and emotional support during times of crisis. All of these various factors reduce the effects of trauma and may therefore reduce your chances of getting PTSD.

Can the values of my community affect my risk of developing PTSD?

Yes. The way your community supports or rejects its victims definitely influences how you may be affected by trauma. If, for example, you are sexually assaulted within a community that understands that women do not ask to be raped, you will be likely to receive competent and kind medical care and psychological support, and PTSD will be less likely to occur. The reverse is true if the sexual assault occurs within a community that shuns or scorns its victims.

I have PTSD but no risk factors. How could that be?

Risk factors are helpful, but they don't identify everybody who is vulnerable to trauma. We are all potentially vulnerable.

Why is it that most people don't develop PTSD after a serious trauma?

Although we've identified a variety of risk factors, there is much we don't know about why some people go on to develop PTSD and others don't. Our general belief is that anyone is at risk if exposed to an adequately serious trauma. As has been postulated since the time of Freud, however, there does seem to be a stress-resistant personality. It would appear that these stress-resistant personalities are more able to withstand serious trauma. According to our theory, the withstanding of trauma requires an ability to avoid the helplessness and numbness that contributes to PTSD. In his book *Post-Traumatic Stress Disorder: The Victim's Guide to Healing and Recovery,* Raymond Flannery has summarized a variety of findings to come up with what he calls a "stress-resistant personality."

What is this stress-resistant personality?

Stress-resistant people tend to be adept problem solvers and have an ability to see meaning in their lives. They tend to be able to keep their cool during difficult situations. They are able to develop and maintain interpersonal relationships. These skills can be summarized as mastery, meaning, and attachment. We'll discuss each of these.

What is the skill of mastery?

Mastery can be seen to include three important factors. One is the ability to take personal control of difficult situations. Another is the ability to make good lifestyle choices, including maintaining a balanced diet, a regular exercise schedule, and time for relaxation. Another is the ability to maintain a sense of humor when things get rough. In addition, Flannery has observed that individuals who demonstrate mastery have a specific way of responding to problems. First, they identify the problem and then gather all the information available to solve the problem. They then reflect on all the possible strategies for a solution and finally implement the strategy that they find to be best. They also have the ability to evaluate what they have done, assessing overall effectiveness and attempting something different if need be. But mastery involves more than just problem solving; it also includes the ability to identify those problems which can and should be solved. You may be familiar with the "Serenity Prayer," integral to Twelve-Step programs but often found hanging on office walls as a source of inspiration: "Grant me the strength to accept the things I cannot change, the courage to change the things I can, and the wisdom to know the difference." Those who have the skill of mastery have this wisdom.

What is the skill of attachment?

The skill of attachment means the ability to cultivate and maintain caring relationships with family, friends and coworkers. Although caring relationships can provide us with emotional and even financial support during difficult times, studies have also shown that on a physiological level, all our bodily systems appear to work more effectively when we are positively involved with other people. The skill of attachment does not only mean having good interpersonal relationships. It also means being committed to projects that give you a reason to live. Such projects might include having a meaningful career, raising a family, or fighting for a cause you believe in. To prevent PTSD, it is often critical to find meaning in the activity that your are participating in during the trauma. If you can find meaning and attachment during war or during a natural disaster, you become somewhat protected from PTSD.

What is the skill of meaning?

In the face of trauma, some people are able to find a deep sense of meaning in their activities. This may be a spiritual belief, or it may be a powerful belief in the importance of family members, work, or country. When disaster strikes, such people have the ability to put the traumatic event into a larger context and are able to turn tragic circumstances into opportunities for growth.

Are these skills something you are born with, or are they learned?

For the most part, coping skills are learned as we grow up. We learn primarily from watching how our parents or other primary caregivers react to and cope with stress. We also learn from our teachers, our friends, the media, and the world around us. A child who grows up in a healthy, supportive home environment is more likely to learn good coping skills than one who is exposed to the confusion and chaos of a dysfunctional home, where one or both parents may be alcoholic or abusive.

Can these skills be learned as an adult if they were not learned as a child?

Yes, that's the good news. While these skills are a sign of optimal physical and mental health, most people have these skills to some degree, and we can all work to improve them. There are many therapists, support groups, and self-help books available to help you learn to master these necessary skills.

Is it possible to have these skills and then to lose them?

Yes. Trauma tends to erode the skills of all of us. The most healthy of us may be able to use their skills to transcend traumatic situations, but almost anyone can be broken down by prolonged, intense trauma. When PTSD does develop, treatment must involve learning or relearning these skills of gaining mastery, attachment, and a sense of meaning.

Are stress-resistant people immune to being affected by trauma?

No. No one is immune. If the situation is bad enough, everyone is at risk.

References

Robin, R. W., B. Chester, et al. "Prevalence and Characteristics of Trauma and Post-Traumatic Stress Disorder in a Southwestern American Indian Community." *American Journal of Psychiatry* 154:11, Nov. 1997, pp. 1582–1588.

Raymond B. Flannery, Jr., Ph.D. *Post-Traumatic Stress Disorder: The Victim's Guide to Healing and Recovery.* New York: Crossroads Publishing, 1992.

Chapter 3

DIAGNOSIS AND SYMPTOMS OF PTSD

How is PTSD diagnosed?

PTSD develops as a consequence of an overwhelming experience, and people with PTSD demonstrate the impact of this trauma in characteristic ways. They may reexperience the trauma, avoid places and situations that remind them of the trauma, or experience bodily changes set off by environmental stimuli that are somehow connected to the trauma. A severe enough trauma will cause some of these symptoms in most people. Later in this chapter these symptoms will be described in greater detail.

A diagnosis of PTSD is made after your situation and symptoms have been carefully considered and compared to the set of definitive criteria set forth in the DSM-IV (see the following pages). A diagnosis of PTSD is determined by a licensed medical professional, but by learning and reading about the condition, you should be able to make an initial assessment yourself. You should also be able to determine whether or not the symptoms you are experiencing warrant professional intervention. If, however, you are unsure or concerned about your symptoms, it would be beneficial for you to seek outside help.

DIAGNOSTIC CRITERIA FOR 309.81
POST-TRAUMATIC STRESS DISORDER

A. The person has been exposed to a traumatic event in which both of the following were present:

1. the person experienced, witnessed, or was confronted with an event or events that involved actual or threatened death or serious injury, or a threat to the physical integrity of self or others

2. the person's response involved intense fear, helplessness, or horror.

Note: In children, this may be expressed instead by disorganized or agitated behavior.

B. The traumatic event is persistently reexperienced in one (or more) of the following ways:

1. recurrent and intrusive distressing recollections of the event, including images, thoughts, or perceptions. *Note:* In young children, repetitive play may occur in which themes or aspects of the trauma are expressed.

2. recurrent distressing dreams of the event. *Note:* In children, there might be frightening dreams without recognizable content.

3. acting or feeling as if the traumatic event were recurring (includes a sense of reliving the experience, illusions, hallucinations, and dissociative flashback episodes, including those that occur on awakening or when intoxicated). *Note:* In young children, trauma-specific reenactment may occur.

4. intense psychological distress at exposure to internal or external cues that symbolize or resemble an aspect of the traumatic event.

5. physiological reactivity on exposure to internal or external cues that symbolize or resemble an activity of the traumatic event.

C. Persistent avoidance of stimuli associated with the trauma and numbing of general responsiveness (not present before the trauma), as indicated by three (or more) of the following:

1. efforts to avoid thoughts, feelings, or conversations associated with the trauma

2. efforts to avoid activities, places, or people that arouse recollections of the trauma

3. inability to recall an important aspect of the trauma

4. markedly diminished interest or participation in significant activities

5. feeling of detachment or estrangement from others

6. restricted range of affect (e.g., unable to have loving feelings)

7. sense of a foreshortened future (e.g., does not expect to have a career, marriage, children, or a normal life span)

D. Persistent symptoms of increased arousal (not present before the trauma), as indicated by two (or more) of the following:

1. difficulty falling asleep

2. irritability or outbursts of anger

3. difficulty concentrating

4. hypervigilance

5. exaggerated startle response

E. Duration of the disturbance (symptoms in Criteria B, C, and D) is more than one month.

F. The disturbance causes clinically significant distress or impairment in social, occupational, or other important areas of functioning.

Specify if:

Acute: if duration of symptoms is less than three months

Chronic: if duration of symptoms is three months or more

Specify if:

With Delayed Onset: if onset of symptoms is at least six months after the stressor

---

* Reprinted with permission from the *Diagnostic and Statistical Manual of Mental Disorder,* Fourth Edition, Washington, DC: American Psychiatric Association, 1994.

Are there different kinds of PTSD?

Yes. The diagnostic manual of psychiatry describes three types of PTSD: acute, chronic, and delayed-onset. As you will learn in later chapters, treatment for each type may vary. In addition, there is an acute stress disorder that may contain all the symptoms of PTSD but has lasted less than one month. While not as disabling as PTSD, acute stress disorders frequently develop into PTSD and should be promptly addressed.

PTSD is considered to be acute if symptoms persist for longer than one month but less than three months. Chronic PTSD has persisted for at least three months. If PTSD develops months or years after the traumatic event, it is considered delayed-onset. Delayed-onset PTSD can be very confusing, since a variety of serious symptoms can develop years after the trauma and after years of normal functioning. Often, delayed-onset PTSD develops in the course of psychotherapy, or when external circumstances allow greater freedom and safety, or when external changes become increasingly stressful. It may be obvious that repeated trauma could precipitate delayed-onset PTSD, but it also seems to be true that a greater sense of safety and openness can allow previously repressed memories to come to the surface, causing symptoms of post-traumatic stress.

What are the other requirements for a PTSD diagnosis?

According to the DSM-IV, there are four different requirements for a diagnosis of PTSD, in addition to the requirement that symptoms last at least one month.

The first requirement is a precipitating traumatic event that led to intense fear, helplessness, or horror. The person might have experienced the trauma directly or might have just witnessed it, but the event must have involved actual or threatened death or serious injury, or a threat to someone's physical integrity.

In addition to the trauma, what symptoms are necessary for a PTSD diagnosis?

The symptoms associated with PTSD are divided into three main categories. For someone to get a diagnosis of PTSD, he or she must have symptoms from each of these three categories: reexperiencing, avoidance/numbing, and increased arousal. One of the complex aspects of the PTSD diagnosis is that there are a variety of symptoms that fit each of these general categories. The symptoms must also persist for longer than a month and be severe enough to inhibit the person's ability to function normally or to enjoy the pleasures of life.

What do you mean by reexperiencing trauma?

Although the initial situation has passed, people with PTSD continue to experience the traumatic event as though it is still occurring. This can be compared to the phantom pains experienced by patients who have had their limbs amputated but continue to feel pain and sensation in the space where their limb had once been.

What are some examples of reexperiencing the trauma?

There are many ways that the traumatic event can be reexperienced. The experience can appear vividly real, as in the case of flashbacks. A person having a flashback feels as though the original trauma is occurring. For example, a war veteran might dive for cover upon hearing a car backfire, fearing an air raid. As he dives for cover, he might feel a host of physiological reactions, such as a rapid heartbeat and profuse sweating. He might begin to panic, feeling and behaving as though he were in the middle of a war. Flashbacks are one unpleasant way to reexperience the traumatic event, though there are others. For example, many people have nightmares about the event. Some people don't remember these nightmares, though their bed partners might comment on their habit of thrashing around in bed, sometimes even shouting or acting out aspects of the trauma. Such nightmares are one reason for insomnia, though PTSD can affect sleep directly, as can anxiety and depression. Other people with PTSD have intrusive, disturbing recollections of the trauma, sometimes spinning the event over and over in their minds. People with PTSD often feel intense distress when reminded of the traumatic event in some way. This reminder can be obvious or extremely subtle, and the distress can be either psychological or physiological. All of these are intrusive symptoms, and they can start after what seems to be a minor reminder or trigger.

What are triggers?

Anything that evokes a feeling or memory of the original trauma is called a trigger. Because each person's experience of trauma is unique, triggers are highly individual, meaning that each person has his own unique set. In situations where whole groups of people have experienced similar trauma, such as Vietnam veterans or survivors of the Oklahoma City bombings, some common triggers may exist (such as a reaction to sudden loud noises). On the whole, however, triggers tend to be personally specific.

Triggers can be people, places, anniversaries, smells, weather conditions, or foods. They can also be emotional situations, items of clothing, or any other situation reminiscent of the trauma. For example, if a child is repeatedly molested in a light blue bedroom, he or she may always have an adverse reaction to a blue room, or even to the color blue itself. Anniversary reactions are common too. As the anniversary date of the original event draws near, victims may find themselves exhibiting symptoms of distress.

Why do these intrusive symptoms occur?

No one knows for sure why intrusive symptoms occur. It is felt, however, that they are a way to make sense of the trauma, to master the situation through repetition. In PTSD, however, this mechanism of understanding and mastery seems to break down. Instead of helping to develop a sense of control, these intrusive symptoms just go on and on.

Does having flashbacks mean that I am going crazy?

No, you are not going crazy, although it may feel like you are. Intrusive symptoms can feel totally out of your

control, and it does take some effort to regain a sense
of equilibrium and mastery.

Is it possible to have intrusive symptoms without a recollection of having been traumatized in the past?

Yes. After being traumatized, your mind will sometimes try to protect you from additional stress by
blocking out some, or all, of your memories of the
event. Even if they are out of your conscious awareness, however, they still exist. Under such circumstances your intrusive symptoms may be experienced as
nonverbal memories.

What are nonverbal memories?

They are recollections that are physical rather than
mental. They may be the creepy sensation of hands being all over your body or a paralysis that may suddenly
afflict you. Nonverbal memories frequently reflect experiences that occurred before you developed language
skills, though they can stem from any period of your
life.

How can I have memories that I've completely forgotten about?

In order to get through the day, we routinely put lots of
information on the back burner. Give it some thought,
and you'll realize that you are conscious of only a small
percentage of the things that you have stored in your
brain. Much of this repressed information is harmless
and is repressed only because we can't be conscious of
everything at once. If we were recalling the name of our
eighth-grade gym teacher while also mulling over a recent trauma, recalling the smile of our favorite aunt
and thinking about cooking dinner, the location of our
dentist, and the name of the presidential candidates,

while also pondering the other million possible items we've ever experienced or known, we'd never get anything done.

The brain is good at a variety of things, including repressing information that isn't immediately useful. It is also good at repressing information that is unpleasant. Normally, however, we allow a controllable amount of unpleasant information to escape this repression so that we can digest the pain and put the unpleasant experience to rest. In PTSD the trauma has overwhelmed this ability to digest controllable amounts of information. Instead, emotionally powerful memories seem to get stuck and are not digested. They remain stored up in our brain, and from time to time, repeated, intrusive "reexperiences" spill out. That is, we continue to relive aspects of the trauma over and over again. Usually those reexperiences are within a recognizable memory. Sometimes the reexperiences are in the form of nonverbal memories. It doesn't much matter. Regardless of whether or not you qualify for a PTSD diagnosis, you should seek some kind of treatment if you are reexperiencing a trauma.

So reexperiencing is the first symptom of PTSD. You said that avoidance and numbing were the second. What do "avoidance" and "numbness" mean, and why are they listed together?

Avoidance and numbness are ways to not experience the enormity of the pain. While they are somewhat different, they tend to accomplish the same thing.

What do you mean by "avoidance"?

Victims of trauma will often go out of their way to avoid thoughts, feelings, or activities that remind them of the traumatic event. Even things that may appear insignificant may be avoided because they are reminis-

cent of the trauma and may induce painful emotions or
physiological reactions. Avoidance can lead to an inability to recall important aspects of the event, for example, because even the recollection can be painful.

How could avoidance behavior affect my life?

In the pursuit of safety and reliability, avoidance behavior reduces pleasure and flexibility. Though they
may not be fully aware of what they are doing, people
with PTSD frequently become constricted in their feelings and experiences. For example, after a serious traffic accident, Bill went through a series of behavior
changes that limited his life. Initially he became frightened to drive unless it was absolutely necessary. He
then gradually became unable to leave his immediate
neighborhood and became quite lonely and isolated.
His social life dried up, and he eventually became quite
depressed and pessimistic. Treatment was necessary to
reverse his cycle of constriction and avoidance.

That example seemed fairly obvious. I think I have PTSD, and my life has become quite constricted, but I don't know exactly what I'm avoiding.

It is fairly common for people with PTSD to have a
fuzzy set of reasons for their avoidance behaviors. You
may not know why red cars make you panic, or why
you are unable to spend the night in a motel. All you
know is that they cause you to feel bad and must therefore be avoided at all costs.

What do you mean by "numbness"?

During times of physical trauma, the body releases certain chemicals that act as natural analgesics. This is a
protective mechanism that enables us to do what needs
to be done to ensure our survival. You have probably

heard or read of situations such as a mountain climber being able to walk for miles on a broken leg. In such an instance the enormous stress led to the production of a natural painkiller, which saved the mountain climber's life. Severe psychological stress produces the same painkiller. In PTSD the painkiller seems to have gotten stuck in the "on" position, and people feel numb long after the trauma has ended. This sort of numbness can lead to diminished interest or participation in activities and may lead to detachment from loved ones. Numbness can rob you of your zest for the future and the present.

What are some of the emotions that can become "shut off" during times of trauma?

Terror, anger, sadness, guilt, and helplessness are all feelings evoked by trauma that can be "shut off" by the mind to help increase your chances of survival.

What are the long-term effects of numbing?

You may feel emotionally dead inside, like you have no feelings at all, or you may only be able to experience certain emotions, such as rage and resentment, and not those of love or tenderness. If you are unable to feel love or tenderness, it will be difficult to develop and maintain intimate personal relationships, and these relationships are essential to your emotional well-being. In addition, you may be unable to feel appropriate emotions at appropriate times. For example, you may feel irritable and find yourself snapping at people you care about, or work with, for no apparent reason. Anger, resentment, and hatred repel other people and can destroy even the most stable relationships. Thus, victims of trauma can find themselves alienated from those they love.

So the first two symptoms are reexperiencing and avoidance/numbing. What do you mean by the last symptom, "increased arousal"?

At the time of the trauma, a typical physical and emotional defense is to become intensely alert and aroused. This is an effective and reasonable defense against danger. In PTSD, signs of increased arousal continue well after the danger has passed. People with PTSD tend to have a variety of related symptoms, including difficulty falling or staying asleep; irritability or outbursts of anger; difficulty concentrating; hypervigilance; and an exaggerated startled response.

Are these symptoms interrelated?

Yes. People suffering from PTSD live as though trapped in a never-ending cycle of symptoms. Triggers in the environment may stimulate the reexperience of trauma, which might, in turn, evoke the symptoms of increased arousal. The pain of increased arousal can lead to avoidance behaviors and increased psychic numbing. Avoidance and numbing are never adequate to control all of the symptoms or avoid all the triggers, and the cycle starts all over again. Unless the condition is diagnosed and treated, the circle of symptoms will continue to revolve.

I'm not sure I can differentiate between the different types of reaction to trauma. Would you give some examples?

Julie was raped six weeks ago. For several weeks she had nightmares, intense anxiety, and recurrent memories of the attack. She noticed that she was no longer able to go jogging every day (an activity that she used to love) because she was afraid of being alone. She was also hesitant to go to work because one of her coworkers reminded her of the rapist. She found herself unable to sleep and was often irritable with friends. She immediately joined a support group for rape survivors and also decided to start seeing her psychotherapist again (something she had discontinued one year earlier). After three weeks she realized that she was feeling better, that most of her symptoms had faded. She was still a bit apprehensive about jogging, but she was able to go running with friends. She realized she had no trouble going to work but was a bit apprehensive about working late, when most of her coworkers had gone home. Six weeks after the rape, Julie was occasionally sad and tearful, but she appeared to be on the road to recovery.

Did Julie have PTSD?

No. She had an acute stress disorder. While she had symptoms of reexperiencing (nightmares), avoidance (avoiding her daily jogs), and increased arousal (being sleepless and irritable), her symptoms had essentially faded within a month. Julie's situation is fairly common. Although the sexual assault was severely traumatic, she was able to seek treatment aggressively and was fortunate in having never been previously traumatized and having a supportive network of friends and families.

Would you give another example?

Mary was driving two of her best friends to work when she skidded on a slippery section of the highway and hit an overpass. Mary was uninjured, but her friends were killed. After the accident, Mary was barely able to function. Frequently tearful, she kept thinking about details of the accident and figuring out ways that she could have prevented the whole thing. She felt enormous guilt, which came out in the nightmares that she had every night. She refused to drive her car because she feared another accident, and was unable to go to work. She felt so bad that she refused to even answer her telephone, much less talk to any of her other friends. These symptoms were not only present after six weeks, they seemed to be getting worse.

Does Mary qualify for a PTSD diagnosis?

Yes. Because her symptoms have persisted for over a month, her diagnosis would be acute PTSD. It is never completely clear why one person gets better and another does not, but Julie may have quickly recovered because she sought help immediately following her trauma, while Mary did not. Another factor is that Mary felt enormous guilt, because she was driving the car. Guilt is a common stumbling block in recoveries.

How about another example?

Jim enlisted in the Vietnam War in 1968 and served for eighteen months. His experiences in Vietnam were, he thought, very similar to those of his army colleagues. Nevertheless, he is haunted by his experiences and has never talked to anyone about what he did, not even his family. He experiences flashbacks, never sleeps well, and has learned that drinking alcohol numbs the intensity of his pain. Although thirty years have passed since the war, his symptoms remain unchanged. His ex-wife considers him an alcoholic who is irritable and self-involved.

What diagnosis does Jim have?

Because his symptoms have persisted for an extended period of time, Jim is said to have chronic PTSD.

I've never slept well my whole life and everybody sees me as uptight, but since I got engaged I seem to be

having more problems than ever before. It creeps me out when my fiancé touches me. Loud noises at night drive me into a panic, and I keep having feelings that I'm dirty or poisoned. It doesn't make any sense, because as far as I can remember, I've never been traumatized. Could I have PTSD?

It's not clear. Your symptoms fit PTSD, but the diagnosis does require a precipitating trauma. It is possible that getting close to your fiancé has stimulated some forgotten trauma from your childhood. People who have your symptoms are often helped by therapy that explores issues in a general way. It may be that you have delayed-onset PTSD, but only time will tell.

If I'm getting evaluated for PTSD, will I need to have a physical examination?

It may or may not be necessary to get a physical examination. If you've been physically assaulted or raped, you should get a physical examination done immediately. Similarly, if your trauma involved some sort of personal illness, your physical well-being should be closely followed. Feeling better physically can help you feel better mentally. In addition, there are some physical illnesses that cause anxiety and depression. A thorough physical examination may help pinpoint what is ailing you.

What about blood tests?

There are no blood tests to diagnose PTSD. Some physical problems can mimic some PTSD symptoms, however, so your doctor may want to do some blood tests to rule out those conditions as being the source of your problems. Thyroid disease can cause depression and anxiety, for example, and so thyroid tests may be necessary.

What mental health disorders can be associated with trauma?

Depression, anxiety, eating disorders, compulsive gambling or spending, amnesia, panic disorders, certain phobias, suicidal feelings, self-mutilating tendencies, delinquent or criminal behaviors, and psychosomatic illnesses are all examples of conditions whose roots can be directly traced back to a precipitating traumatic event. All of these conditions can also occur with PTSD. A diagnosis of one of these disorders does not rule out a diagnosis of any of the others. In addition, some of the above disorders can predispose you to the type of trauma that could lead to PTSD. If you are a thrill-seeking, impulsive substance abuser, for example, you are much more likely to get involved in traffic accidents, fights, and criminal activity, each of which could lead to PTSD.

What about alcoholism and drug addiction?

Addiction to alcohol or drugs can develop out of an initial need or desire to self-medicate in order to cope with the aftereffects of trauma. You may start drinking to drown your sorrows, for example, or to feel more confident in social situations or to be intimate with lovers. The initial intent might have been reasonable, but can lead to addictive behavior. In the same way, some people may use alcohol and illicit substances to try to quell some of the symptoms of PTSD. For example, alcohol, Valium, and heroin are sometimes used to subdue symptoms of increased arousal, just as cocaine and other stimulants are sometimes used to alleviate numbing. Unfortunately, however, overuse of alcohol or drugs often becomes a problem in itself. As you become dependent on the substance, in addition to your symptoms of trauma, you subsequently develop debilitating symptoms related exclusively to your addiction.

In addition, substance abuse can contribute to the initial development of PTSD by interfering with the mind's ability to think clearly and process relevant information. Half the people in addiction recovery programs have been found to be victims of childhood abuse, just as half of the Vietnam veterans with PTSD have some form of chemical dependency. Drugs and PTSD don't mix well.

I feel depressed almost all the time. Could it be a related to PTSD?

Yes, most definitely. Statistics show that about 50 percent of those people with PTSD exhibit the symptoms of depression. Clinical depression, one of the most common psychiatric illnesses in the country, has many contributing factors. Related to our biochemistry, our psychology, and our environment, its onset can be triggered by many things, including grief, divorce, chronic illness, loneliness, financial difficulties, retirement, and various other life transitions. Loss tends to be the foremost cause, though depression sometimes occurs without a clear reason. Victims of PTSD are highly susceptible to developing depression because of the magnitude of the losses, both physical and spiritual, that they have sustained.

Depression is characterized by a loss of energy and a lack of interest in life. It feels as though you are stuck in the middle of a thick, dark cloud with no visible means of escape. You may feel sad or tearful, or overcome with such a deep sense of helplessness that even the simple task of getting up in the morning becomes impossible. However, as with alcoholism and other mental health disorders, depression can help cause PTSD, can be caused by PTSD, or can develop alongside PTSD.

Can medical problems be attributed to trauma?

Yes. Studies have proven that a variety of medical conditions can be related to stress and trauma. These include headaches, rashes, backaches, stomach problems and susceptibility to colds and flu, diabetes, hypertension, and even heart conditions. They can often be a direct consequence of the physiological problems created by PTSD. For example, if you are always tense, deprived of sleep, and haunted by memories, it is very likely that you will suffer from headaches. If your immune system is compromised by constant stress, frequent colds and other illnesses are also common. The constant outpouring of distress hormones can raise your blood pressure and lead to heart disease. It is important to be aware that sometimes a traumatic injury to the head can cause symptoms such as chronic headaches, backaches, memory loss, and periods of disorientation. These symptoms, although due to a traumatic injury, are not symptoms of PTSD. At the same time, people who have suffered mild head injuries often do develop PTSD. As we've said, it may take an expert to tease apart your symptoms and come up with the most useful diagnosis or set of diagnoses.

Can self-injurious behavior be attributed to PTSD?

Yes. Many people who have PTSD cut and burn themselves. This sort of behavior is especially scary and confusing, both to the victim and to the victim's friends and family. There are several things to know about self-mutilating behavior. First, cutting and burning are usually not attempts at suicide. Instead, they are efforts to control the pain of the trauma. For many, the cutting or burning is an expression of their self-loathing, a feeling that is common after trauma that may be considered shameful, such as incest. Self-mutilation may also be a way to show the people around you that you are injured, that there is something wrong even though you have no obvious injuries. Other people go to great lengths to avoid discovery. For them, the self-injury may serve a self-numbing function. When we inflict controllable pain on ourselves, our body produces natural painkillers, and we tend to go somewhat numb. You might remember that numbness is a cardinal symptom of PTSD, and it may feel especially tempting to inflict pain in order to reliably feel this numbing and distancing. Self-injury is particularly common in children who have been abused, but it occurs with many people with a variety of psychological problems, including PTSD. As we will make more clear in the chapters on treatment, numbing is a defense that is limited in its effectiveness. In fact, numbness tends to help in the very short run and perpetuate and deepen the PTSD in the long run. If you are hurting yourself in order to "self-medicate" some aspect of your pain, be aware that there are ways to remove the injurious behavior and remove the psychological pain. You don't have to perpetuate this cycle.

I was sexually abused as a child and also have a problem with throwing up my food. Despite my efforts, I keep gaining weight. Are these two problems related?

Many people with PTSD also have an eating disorder. When you say that you throw up your food, it probably means you have bulimia. Actually, bulimia consists of a cycle of behaviors, not just vomiting. People with bulimia almost always start off wanting to be thin, which leads to dieting. Dieting leads to starvation, which leads to overwhelming hunger, which leads to overeating, which leads to purging (vomiting or laxatives), which leads to rage at yourself, which leads back to dieting. The cycle can restart itself indefinitely. As with PTSD, efforts to control yourself or the surrounding world backfire, and you are left more out of control than you were in the beginning. Bulimia is very common among people with PTSD, especially among women who have been abused. One recent study found, for example, that half of the patients being treated for bulimia had been physically or sexually abused.

During the traumatic event, I felt as though I was in a dream, like I was watching it all happening to someone else. Since then, I frequently feel like I'm going through life in a dream. What's going on?

You are probably experiencing an altered state of consciousness known as dissociation. It's a form of "tuning out" that enables the victim to endure a severe trauma in a dreamlike state. Dissociation may be effective during an uncontrollable event, such as childhood sexual abuse or an uncontrollable battle scene. Like the other PTSD defenses, dissociation is useful at the time of the trauma. Afterwards, however, people tend to use this defense to respond to any sort of threat or anxiety. Dissociation may be fine to deal with an uncontrollable situation, but it works poorly in most of the experiences of everyday life. Dissociation may conceal real warning signs of impending danger and it may delay effective action, and it always prevents sharp, realistic evaluation of the situation.

It seems that some people are perpetual victims. Is this a coincidence?

It may be a coincidence, but people with PTSD tend to approach the world in ways that can bring about further trauma. They may, for example, use the psychological defense of dissociation. While they may not be consciously aware of using such a defense, dissociation impairs the ability to foresee danger and make efforts to prevent it. In fact, any of the cardinal symptoms of PTSD can lead to further traumatization. For example, if you have a strong tendency to reexperience the trauma, you may feel retraumatized by an event that would not have been considered traumatic prior to the original one. If overarousal leads you to feeling irritable and rageful, you stand a greater chance of being involved in confrontations that can lead to physical fights.

There are many types of examples. As we've mentioned, thrill-seeking, drug-abusing teenagers may put themselves at risk for trauma every night that they go out driving with their friends. People who have suffered long-term physical or sexual abuse tend to choose friends and lovers who re-create the abusive situation. Someone who grew up with an alcoholic parent is likely to re-create relationships with other alcoholic people, where a cycle of codependency and unhappy chaos is perpetuated. We all tend to choose familiar relationships. If your familiar relationships tended to be abusive in some way, you are definitely at risk for continuing this cycle.

What keeps some people trapped in perpetually traumatic situations?

For some, leaving is not a realistic option. Children, soldiers, and ghetto dwellers have limited opportunities to escape their traumatic situations. As we point out throughout the book, the first step in the treatment of PTSD is the acquisition of safety. For some, this may not be possible for an extended period of time.

Other people are trapped by a combination of psychology and security. We see this most clearly in adult victims of domestic abuse. For example, Rosie's husband beat her on a fairly regular basis, usually on the weekends after he'd had a few drinks at the local bar.

She wanted to leave him, but how could she support the kids and herself? Further, her husband was always apologetic after the fights, and then they felt even closer than before. She hoped the the fights would just go away. And despite it all, Rosie knew that she still loved her husband. He reminded her of her father. And she believed she'd never find anybody better. Rosie's situation is typical. Her self-esteem and self-supporting skills have been squashed in the marriage, and she puts up with trauma in order to keep the relationship going. We don't know enough about Rosie to say for sure, but she may have developed a "traumatic bond" with her husband. Traumatic bonding occurs when victims internalize the value systems of their perpetrators. Also known as "identification with the aggressor," traumatic bonding allows the development of strong emotional attachments toward abusers. This was demonstrated in a famous case in Stockholm. Hostages were taken during a bank robbery, and these captives ended up aligning themselves with the robbers. This concept of traumatic bonding came to be known as the Stockholm Syndrome. While it holds true for bank robberies, we see it far more frequently in domestic violence or in any form of trauma that is prolonged.

Can victims of trauma become abusive themselves?

Yes. As we mentioned above, "identification with the aggressor" is a powerful psychological mechanism that leads the vulnerable person to take on some of the characteristics of the person who is hurting them. For example, many victims of child abuse grow up to be child abusers themselves. It is interesting to note that this phenomenon is also found in less traumatic situations, as in company employees who take on certain of the destructive characteristics of their boss. In fact, identification with powerful figures is a very common experience.

What happened to me wasn't my fault. Why am I being blamed?

Blame-the-victim attitudes have long been pervasive in our society. Grass-roots efforts to protect the victim have led to a reversal of this trend in the United States, but it is still fairly common for victims to be met with scorn and disbelief when they attempt to tell their stories. One explanation for this behavior is society's need to deny the fact that human beings are capable of committing atrocities on a regular basis. As Rebecca Coffey has asserted in her book *Unspeakable Truths and Happy Endings,* it is easier and safer to side with the perpetrators. In addition, acknowledging the reality of trauma implies that we too could be victimized. For that reason, it helps to believe that the victim must have been at least partly responsible for what happened. Few people want to admit the possibility of such helplessness.

Veterans returning from Vietnam were met with this kind of attitude. The society to which they returned was disillusioned with the war and wanted to forget all about it. By blaming the returning soldiers for the war and by believing that they got what they deserved, society attempted to put the whole nasty affair behind them.

Nobody is blaming me, as far as I can see, but I still feel totally guilty about what happened. Why is that?

You may be suffering from a form of guilt that is more difficult to understand. We all carry around within us a mechanism for judging ourselves. For some of us this judging is too strict. For others it's too lax. For most of us this self-judging mechanism fluctuates a good bit but is essentially reasonable. You might have noticed such a self-judging mechanism within yourself. It often feels like a voice that is observing and criticizing your actions and doesn't quite feel like a part of you. This is entirely normal. After a terrible trauma, however, we tend to become less emotionally flexible, and this self-judging mechanism can become quite strict. It might scrutinize your actions and obsess about ways you could have avoided the trauma. It might decide that you could have prevented the trauma or that you encouraged the trauma in the first place. This self-judging mechanism might take the side of the perpetrator and inflict even more pain on you. This unconscious guilt is often more painful and disabling than any kind of criticism from other people; after all, who knows your weak points better than you yourself? Part of recovery is to learn to accept and forgive yourself. At this moment, though, this may be difficult for you to do.

I have some of the symptoms of PTSD but not all of them. Does that mean I have PTSD?

To qualify for the PTSD diagnosis, you need to have had the trauma and been affected for at least a month. You must also have symptoms from each of the three categories: avoidance, reexperiencing, and arousal. If your symptoms do not meet these criteria, you don't officially qualify for the diagnosis. If you are suffering, however, you need to find a way to help yourself or to secure help from others. Much of the rest of this book should still be useful to you.

Is PTSD easy to diagnose?

It may be. If you have had an obviously serious trauma and are suffering lots of symptoms, a skilled professional should have no problem with the diagnosis. For victims of prolonged or repeated trauma, however, diagnosis may be more difficult. In such cases, it is not unusual for victims to present themselves for treatment because they are suffering from a variety of related conditions, including insomnia, depression, anxiety, physical problems, and emotional or relationship problems. It may take weeks of work to begin to uncover the sources of the symptoms. Victims of childhood abuse may not remember the incident, or may be in denial of the meaning of the memories. For others, abuse may have become so frequent that the victim believes that their frequent traumas are just part of daily life. This is particularly true for victims of domestic violence.

I have noticed that my husband jumps at the slightest noise and is always looking over his shoulder. Why is he so afraid? I am the one who was raped.

It is not uncommon for persons who are closest to the victim to be so shocked and shaken by the event that they themselves develop stress-related symptoms. A study done on the partners of rape victims demonstrated that one third had intrusive, recurrent thoughts about rape and more than half exhibited signs of hypervigilance. The study also found that most experienced severe feelings of powerlessness and helplessness related to the fact that they blamed themselves for not being able to protect their partner from harm. When friends and loved ones develop stress-related symptoms, they are known as covictims and they too may require professional intervention and treatment.

Is it possible to develop symptoms of PTSD if the traumatic event occurred a long time ago?

Yes. Studies on war veterans, crime victims, and incest survivors have demonstrated that years can pass between the occurrence of the traumatic event and the manifestation of obvious symptoms. Time periods of over twenty years have frequently been documented. Symptoms that spontaneously occur after long periods of time can make an accurate diagnosis difficult. One reason is that victims may be surprised by the sudden onset of symptoms after such a long period of time and may be reluctant to consider the connections. In some cases, the victim astutely makes the connection between the development of symptoms and a previous traumatic event, but the therapist has a hard time believing the information that the client brings to the session. If that's the case, you may need to question your therapist's experience in treating PTSD.

Do symptoms ever go away on their own?

Yes, this does happen. People with PTSD may outgrow their symptoms or develop effective coping strategies. But for others, untreated symptoms can persist indefinitely. Studies conducted on Holocaust survivors in 1992 demonstrated that over 50 percent of those interviewed continued to suffer from PTSD fifty years after the event.

References
Coffey, R. *Unspeakable Truths and Happy Endings.* Lutherville, Md.: Sidran Press, 1998.

Diagnostic and Statistical Manual, Volume IV (DSM-IV). Washington, DC: American Psychiatric Association Press, 1994.

Chapter 4

FEELINGS ASSOCIATED WITH PTSD

Which specific feelings and emotions can be associated with PTSD?

PTSD causes a whole host of interconnected feelings, including numbness, anger, loss, fear, shame, self-blame, and helplessness. These crippling feelings have been physiologically and psychologically induced by the traumatic experience. Although the intensity of these feelings may differ from person to person, all victims of trauma experience some, if not all, of these feelings. In this chapter, we will discuss some of the common feelings that are experienced by people with PTSD. In addition, we will describe some ways you can deal with emotions that tend to overwhelm you.

How does trauma affect our emotions?

Prior to the trauma, our emotions served a variety of purposes. They told us when things were going well, for example, and they warned us of danger. With PTSD we lose control over our feelings, and they can become inappropriately intense and inappropriately directed. While we may have periods of normal functioning, PTSD seriously damages our ability to use emotions to make sense of the world. In addition, many emotions are pleasant, and people with PTSD tend to lose their ability to experience even the "good" emotions.

But I don't feel any of these feelings. All I feel is numb. Is numbness a feeling?

It is in a sense. Numbness is probably better seen, however, as a defense to protect yourself from feeling too much. PTSD is associated with overpowering emotions, and numbness is one way you defend yourself from being overwhelmed.

Calling numbness a defense implies that I'm doing it on purpose. But I don't even like numbness. Why do you imply that it's my decision to feel this way?

Emotional defenses are not something you are consciously aware of creating. They are subconscious and you probably have little control over them at this point. It is important to understand, though, that when faced with an overwhelming trauma, our mind and our body can shut off. This can cause us to feel that we are simply observers at the time of the trauma. While we are trying to make sense of what happened, we may also develop this numbing or dissociation after the trauma has occurred. The problem with numbing is that it prevents us from accurately and assertively dealing with our memories and feelings. But when we do let out our feelings, they are often too intense, both to ourselves and to the people around us. A central back-and-forth in PTSD is this rotation between feeling too little and feeling too much.

Does feeling numb mean that I don't have any other feelings?

It's not that you don't have any feelings. Everyone has feelings. Numbness protects you from being overwhelmed by the intensity of the negative feelings evoked by your traumatic experience. It is very likely that some of the painful symptoms you are now experiencing are related to the fact that these feelings have never been confronted and resolved. Therapy can help bring out these suppressed, dangerous feelings in a safe, measured way.

If blocking out negative feelings is a natural defense mechanism against experiencing pain, why would I want to confront them?

That's a question that most people with PTSD ask. Who wants to go around exposing themselves to painful, traumatic feelings? As we will discuss later, dealing with the numbness and avoidance may become central to your recovery of a fuller range of emotional experiences. You may associate emotion only with pain, but there are other emotions out there that are vital to our existence, emotions like love, joy, and intimacy. If you have PTSD, you may be missing out on some of the most precious experiences we can have.

I feel numb occasionally, but what I mostly feel is anger. What's going on?

Everyone feels angry from time to time. It's a normal human emotion, as are feelings of loneliness, anxiety, and sadness. For most people without PTSD, feeling angry is a relatively brief experience and develops in response to a reasonable provocation. For victims of trauma, however, anger can be ever present, bubbling just below the surface, erupting regularly and uncontrollably and leaving a trail of devastation in its wake.

So other people with PTSD have trouble with anger?

Absolutely. Some people wake up in the morning seething with anger, literally unable to go about their business for fear of the havoc that may ensue. Others find themselves flaring up without warning, lashing out at other people because of relatively minor inconveniences. Some respond to these feelings by getting into fights with the people around them, while others take their anger out on themselves.

Is it possible to just get rid of all my anger?

Anger is a reasonable reaction to a perceived threat. While we might like to feel such intense feelings only rarely, it is important to remember that a full human life requires a wide spectrum of emotions, and anger is one of those normal emotions. At the same time, anger is one of the many feelings that get waylaid by PTSD. With the overwhelming trauma, our emotions and effectiveness are crushed. Frustration and anger are powerfully remembered, and, as part of the core PTSD problem, these feelings of frustration and anger are not resolved but instead lurk beneath the surface, constantly threatening to escape. As with the other powerful emotions associated with PTSD, anger is generally not moderate and reasonable. It threatens to overwhelm, and people with PTSD generally try to keep the anger monster submerged. But the anger remains. It might be anger at the traumatic situation, at the perpetrators, at lost opportunities, or at yourself. You might find that instead of dissipating, your anger has gotten worse. Generally speaking, it is impossible to seek adequate revenge against the trauma itself, and we tend to take out our rage and frustration on the people around us. Anger might have begun to dominate your life, costing you work, friends, and loved ones. You may have become a hermit to avoid inflicting your rage on those around you. There is no way to just get rid of your anger, but there are ways to control and modulate such an intense feeling.

How do I deal with my angry feelings?

It is important to learn to manage your anger, just as it's important to manage all of your intense emotions. Anger management is not a cure, but a series of techniques to help you control the way you react to your feelings. Some methods used to control anger include relaxation, exercise, venting, taking time out, and creatively expressing your anger. We'll discuss each of these. In addition, we will amplify them in the treatment chapters.

How does relaxation help?

Learning to soothe and relax yourself during times of intense emotion is vital to your recovery. A state of calm is more conducive to reflection, rational thinking, and effective problem solving than is out-of-control rage. Breathing exercises are an example of a relaxation technique, as are yoga and meditation.

Relaxation techniques can sometimes make you anxious. People with PTSD often live a very tense life, partly as a way to prevent the intrusion of painful memories. If you try to sit quietly for a minute, for example, you may be flooded with anxiety-producing thoughts or memories. If you find that this is the case, you should go slowly with relaxation techniques and should probably consider treatment with a therapist trained in such techniques.

How does exercise help?

Engaging in regular exercise is an extremely useful way to get rid of pent-up emotions and angry feelings. Exercise limbers up our muscles, frees up our minds, and induces a feeling of calmness and well-being. If you find that exercise makes you feel more tense, you might want to reconsider the type of exercise that you do. For our purposes, exercise should be reasonably challenging and fun. People who tend to criticize themselves tend to make exercise into a joyless labor. Part of your recovery from PTSD is to find forms of activity that you enjoy. If it's been a while since you have been physically active, you will probably need to see your doctor for medical clearance. But whatever you do, seek some pleasure in your exercise.

What do you mean by "venting"?

Venting emotion means to let it out, to express your feelings in a reasonable way. As we've said, people with PTSD have trouble following a middle path between too much emotion and too little emotion. In regard to anger, you may have a tendency to rant and rave or you may shut it all up, or you may do both. It is going to be important that you learn how to practice modulation. You might try this with a therapist, since therapists are trained to deal with outpourings of intense emotion. In addition, groups of people who have been similarly traumatized may be able to help you deal with your overwhelming emotions, since they have often been through the same thing.

It is also possible to release pent-up angry feelings by finding a private spot where you can let loose. In your car, in the middle of an open field, anywhere where you can shout it all out without hurting others. Some people find banging things or hitting objects helpful. If this is the case, choose objects that will not cause damage to yourself, to others, or to property. You might find it helpful to beat on a drum or bash a pillow or a punching bag.

What do you mean by "taking time out"?

Taking time out means actively separating yourself from others during or in anticipation of an angry outburst. This gives you the space and time to calm yourself down, clear your head, collect your thoughts and plan a more appropriate course of action. You have probably heard the expression "counting to ten." This is, in effect, a form of taking time out. Here you are actually taking the time to count to ten so that you can put a little psychological distance between yourself and the problem. The development of a sense of perspective is vital to recovery in PTSD, and something as simple as counting to ten can be helpful to many people. For most victims of trauma this is probably not sufficient. It might be better for you to completely remove yourself from the situation and engage in another activity completely. Taking a walk, engaging in exercise or sport, meditating, lifting weights, reading, writing, and painting are all helpful "time-out" activities.

What are ways to creatively express my anger?

You might try coping with anger creatively by painting a picture, writing a story or poem, or engaging in stream-of-consciousness journal writing. Creative dance and improvisational theater techniques are also useful methods of creative expression. Creative expression can give concrete form to intangible, slippery feelings. Creative expression may be seen as a form of venting, though in this case violent feelings are rechanneled into positive artistic expression. Being creative and having something to show for your efforts may feel extremely rewarding. We will discuss creative arts therapies in chapters 7 and 8, where all the treatments are talked about in more depth.

Can medication help with angry feelings?

There is no medication that specifically treats anger, though there are medications that can help relax you. We will discuss such medications in chapter 7. You may find it helpful to discuss this issue with your doctor.

I feel like going out and killing the person who caused this to happen to me! Any suggestions?

Most trauma survivors experience some desire for revenge against whoever or whatever caused their trauma. Some experience mild inklings, but for others the need for vengeance can be all-consuming. It is a powerful emotion, capable of driving nations to war and individuals to commit murder.

If you were dealt a grave injustice, it is normal to be angry and understandable that you want to achieve justice. However, sometimes this is not possible and acting on your emotions would not be in your best interest. For example, suppose your six-year-old daughter was sexually abused and murdered but the man who you believe committed the act was not convicted and continues to live on your block. You may feel that you have a right or an obligation to go out and "do him in." But what good would that do? You would probably spend the rest of your life behind bars, and your little girl would still be dead. If your vengeful feelings are out of control, get help fast before you find yourself in a heap of trouble.

Revenge fantasies, however, need not replay into action. For some people, the mere act of having these fantasies lessens the tension created by the emotion. Daydreaming or fantasizing about revenge in vivid detail can sometimes substitute for action. But if such fantasies are ongoing and appear obsessive, it would be useful to get help.

What about seeking legal recourse?

Although this is not exactly an anger management technique, seeking legal recourse if it is possible, through the courts or by enlisting the help of the police, can be very empowering. Taking the appropriate legal steps, in a formal, methodical way, can help redirect your feelings of anger in a more positive direction. Robbers, rapists, and other assailants can sometimes be caught and brought to trial. In some cases you may even receive a monetary compensation for your losses. However, for many victims, legal recourse may be fruitless, leading to additional anger and frustration.

I never feel safe anymore. Why am I so afraid?

Feeling fear is a normal reaction to trauma. It is also an ongoing symptom in persons who suffer from PTSD. Try to examine your fears. If you are afraid of further trauma, the first thing to establish is whether you are safe from additional harm. In single instances of trauma, such as a hurricane or a serious accident, the chances of a repeat occurrence are probably rare, so your fearful feelings are probably related to physiological changes that occurred at the time of the event. It is normal and understandable for you to be feeling this way, but your feelings are not rational or realistic. However, some victims of trauma, particularly victims of incest or other physical or sexual abuse, continue to live with or associate with their assailants. If this is the case, your fear of repeated trauma is probably justified.

On a psychological level, your experience (regardless of its origin), has most likely left you feeling helpless, powerless, and very vulnerable. Your perception of the world as a safe and secure place may feel shattered. If the harm was inflicted by another person, mistrust can feed your fear. This is especially acute with victims of incest or physical abuse in the home. These feelings, coupled with the physiological state of hyperarousal (whereby your body reacts to even minor environmental stresses or triggers as if in a constant state of alert), are probably the reason why you feel so frightened. In addition, you may also be afraid of your symptoms. Having flashbacks, bursts of uncontrollable anger, or periods of amnesia can be very frightening. You may not know what triggers these reactions and may be afraid of what you might do should one of them occur out of the blue. For example, combat veterans may be constantly afraid of committing acts of violence during a flashback.

What can I do to alleviate my feelings of fear?

We will talk more at length about this in chapter 7, but there are a few principles that specifically relate to the treatment of fear. If you are still living or associating with your assailant, you run the risk of further abuse, so it is very important to try to find a place to live where you can be free from harm. Perhaps you have a family member or friend who would be willing to take you in for a while. If not, there are many shelters and organizations specially geared toward helping victims of domestic abuse. You will find a list of such places at the back of the book. It might be necessary to secure the help of the police department or a counselor or some other mental health professional. There are also ways you can help yourself. If you are a victim of rape, there are many crisis centers that can help you. You may also choose to secure certain safety precautions in your own life. For example, if your house was robbed, you could install an alarm system or reinforce your locks. You might decide to move to a different neighborhood or even take up a course in self-defense.

However, your first step is understanding that your feelings of fear are real and a direct result of your experience and not because you are crazy or paranoid. If you are safe from harm but still experiencing fearful feelings much of the time, it is helpful to try to identify what you are afraid of. If you are afraid of your symptoms, you can try to identify what triggers your reactions. Being able to anticipate when such reactions may occur can help alleviate some of these feelings. However, even though it is normal to feel afraid as a result of your trauma, it is not normal to live your life in constant fear, always looking over your shoulder, always on guard. If you are unable to cope with these feelings on your own, it is important to find someone to help you.

I feel as though this is all my fault. If only I had done things differently . . .

It is very common for victims of trauma to blame themselves or to feel guilty about what happened. These feelings are normal, related in part to a sense of powerlessness inflicted by the traumatic event and in part to the blame-the-victim attitude so pervasive in our society. Victims may blame themselves, feeling that different action on their part could have prevented the situation from occurring. If they hadn't worn that sexy black dress to the party or walked home alone from work, they wouldn't have been raped. If they had been able to respond with action rather than remaining frozen in fear, then perhaps they could have prevented the robber from shooting their coworker. These feelings are based on a premise that their actions played a major role in causing the trauma. This, however, is usually not the case at all. Most acts of trauma are sudden, random events that could not have been prevented, and they are usually fraught with double-bind situations whereby any option taken would result in victims risking their own lives or the lives of others.

Self-blame can also be seen as a form of self-control resulting from situations in which victims felt absolutely powerless—possibly one of the worst feelings a human being can experience. By blaming yourself for the event, you may be attempting to salvage a feeling of control. The idea that there was something that could have been done to prevent the situation is less devastating than coming to terms with the fact that terrible things happen for no reason. Another reason why victims blame themselves is the internalization of cultural or religious attitudes that they have been brought up to believe. The idea that "bad things don't happen to good people," for instance, implies that if something bad does happen, it is probably a punishment for something bad that you have done. Some cultures try to explain away catastrophes as being due to something that happened in another life, or as a result of sins one's ancestors may have committed. These teachings are very destructive to victims of trauma, who were more than likely just in the wrong place at the wrong time.

Survivor guilt is also a form of self-blame. You may feel guilty because you survived while others did not. Or you may feel guilty because you sustained injuries that were less serious or suffered fewer losses. It's a kind of inverted feeling, because there is a sense that if your losses had been greater, perhaps the losses of others would somehow be less.

It is important to realize, however, that it is normal to have these deep feelings of guilt or self-blame. In other words, don't feel guilty about feeling guilty. If you look at the big picture, you will understand why you are feeling this way.

All in all, self-blame is a form of revictimization, as you continue to inflict emotional pain and punishment on yourself.

How do I cope with feelings of guilt and self-blame?

This is often accomplished during the course of treatment, but there are some specific things to bear in mind that directly relate to guilt. First, acknowledge that you are hurting, that something has devastated you and now you are suffering the consequences. Try to look at your behavior during the trauma in a wider context. Was the situation really caused by something that you did or did not do, or in reality, were you doing your best in a no-win situation?

Some victims blame themselves even though they had no way to avoid the trauma. For example, suppose one morning, instead of driving your child to school the way you usually do, you were running late and had her take the bus instead. Suppose the bus gets into an accident, and your child is injured or even killed. You may feel wracked with terrible guilt, blaming yourself for being tired or lazy that morning and not driving your child to school. This kind of guilt, although understandable, is really unfounded. You had no way of knowing that the bus would get into an accident that day. It was a random event over which you had no control.

It is also important to place rape and other crimes into their social context. You were not raped because the dress you were wearing was too short, or because you walked home alone through the park. These facts may suggest some negligence, but crime is a widespread sociological problem and usually occurs regardless of precautions that one may have taken. For example, rape is a crime of violence and aggression and has little to do with sex. Statistics also show that most rapes are not committed by strangers but by people women know, often very well.

Another thing to realize is that our thinking and our perceptions are often distorted by trauma, which affects our ability to correctly assess the situation and to make sound, rational decisions. Thus, even if some of the actions you may have committed during the event were, in retrospect, not the wisest, you need to understand that you were probably doing the best you could under very difficult circumstances.

In some instances, guilt may well be justified. Perhaps others did die or were injured as a result of your deliberate actions or inadvertent negligence. This kind of guilt is much more difficult to deal with, because it will need to involve some form of self-forgiveness. Securing the help of a therapist in such cases would be indicated.

How can I live with myself after the terrible things I did?

Feelings of guilt and shame are very closely connected. You may have been forced to engage in activities that go against your moral, ethical, or religious convictions. Perhaps your were forced to engage in humiliating sexual activities as a child or perhaps you were coerced through love or promises of intimacy into engaging in sexual acts that may even have started out as something thrilling, but went far beyond what you could have imagined. In certain instances you may have even been threatened with death or with additional beatings if you did not comply. In circumstances such as these it is important to understand that you had no choice but to comply in order to survive. When a plane went down in the Andes Mountains about twenty years ago, the survivors of the wreck were forced to resort to eating human flesh in order to survive. Up there in the cold, with no food and little chance of rescue, eating human flesh, however horrible and immoral, was the only alternative to death. Feeling shame when you have suffered some form of indignity or engaged in an activity that goes against your moral or ethical grain is a natural emotion and a common response to feelings of utter helplessness.

I wish that I had been a better wife!

The majority of battered women believe that they could have prevented the abuse from occurring by doing more to keep their abuser satisfied. They think, If only I had taken better care of my body, or kept the house a little cleaner, or been a better cook. These are common justifications made by abused women. But the truth is, even if you had done all of the above, the chances are that the abuse would still have occurred. Abusive spouses do not hit their wives because the house isn't clean enough. They do it because they are damaged individuals behaving in violent, criminal ways.

I feel overwhelmed by feelings of sadness and grief. Will these feelings ever go away?

It is very natural to feel the need to grieve the losses you have endured as a result of your experience. Your losses, whether they are physical, emotional, financial, or even spiritual, are very real. For example, you may have lost friends or family members, the use of parts of your body, your ability to earn a living, your home, your possessions, your virginity, or even your self-confidence or self-esteem. If you were abused as a child, you may feel as though you have lost your childhood, your innocence, or even your right to safety and security. The losses endured by victims of trauma are tremendous and, for some people, never seem to stop adding up. Grieving, however, is an important emotion that paves the way to healing. We all suffer losses throughout our lives, and we must eventually come to terms with them in order to move on. It is a slow process, but most of us are able to eventually let our wounds heal and get on with our lives. For people who suffer from PTSD, however, the normal grieving process is much more difficult. This is primarily because, for them, the traumatic event and the losses associated with the event are reexperienced over and over again. Environmental triggers, secondary wounding, and the biological changes which have occurred not only re-create the situation but cause them to experience their losses with greater intensity.

It feels as though I'm so alone with my grief. Is this perception accurate?

Unfortunately, this may be so. In some societies, people are intolerant when they observe that the grieving process of others continues for longer than what they feel is necessary. In American society, for example, excessive grief is often considered a weakness or a sign of indulging in self-pity, and there is a preference instead for the the stoic attitude of needing to be able to "grin and bear it." This attitude is especially damaging for victims of trauma who have suffered tremendous losses and often feel as though they must carry this burden alone. It has been suggested that this attitude may be due to a fear of suffering, which is easier to deny than to confront.

Your feelings of being alone with your grief may be secondary to feeling different from others, misunderstood, or even flawed in some way. You may even see confirmation of these feelings in the way others are treating you, but be aware that it is very possible for your perceptions to be clouded by PTSD. An important part of the healing process is learning how to reach out appropriately to the people around you. In doing so, you will discover that everyone bears scars and has small flaws and that your experience does not separate you from the rest of the human race.

Can religious institutions be helpful in times of grief?

Yes, all cultures have rituals that are designed to deal with grief. Wakes, memorial services, and funerals are traditional methods of dealing with grief. For example, within the Jewish culture it is recognized that grieving takes at least a year, and the time spent grieving is considered to be essential for health and recovery. In other cultures the grief of the individual is shared by the entire community or acknowledged by rituals designed to comfort the bereaved individual. But most people who have PTSD will have no real use for religious or cultural rituals, because such rituals are usually connected to death and dying, and for many, no one has actually died. If your trauma did not involve death, you may feel that it won't be addressed within traditional religion.

Does this mean that if my trauma did not involve death, a religious institution would be of no help?

No, not necessarily. After suffering a great trauma, most people feel a lot better if they have the comfort of a supportive family, a network of friends, or an institution. If your trauma was an isolating event, as most traumas are, it might be very helpful to make use of the resources within your place of worship. For example, if you have been raped and feel sinful or dirty, it is reasonable to approach your minister, priest, rabbi, or other religious leader and discuss the issue. This may require some extra effort on your part because you probably feel very isolated, but if you do reach out, you may be pleasantly surprised with what you may hear.

I feel better when I am angry than when I am sad.

This is understandable. Anger creates adrenaline surges that enable you to feel strong and powerful, while grief and sadness make you feel weak and powerless. But if you do not grieve for your losses, you are in effect denying that they exist, and until you are able to come to terms with all aspects of your experience, you will not be able to begin the healing process.

What happens when grief is not acknowledged or resolved?

Unfortunately, unresolved grief has been known to lead to the development of many other symptoms and conditions relating to PTSD, including excessive rage; addictions and compulsions; depression; anxiety and panic disorders; a variety of physical conditions such as heart disease and asthma; and even psychosomatic ailments.

Why is grieving important?

Allowing yourself the time to grieve for the losses you sustained during your trauma is a necessary part of healing. Although painful, the process of grieving enables you to examine your losses, to attempt to put them into perspective and to begin to contemplate a future in spite of all you have lost.

Under times of grief and stress we tend to use a characteristic set of defenses against pain. Elisabeth Kubler-Ross in 1969 delineated the grieving process into several recognizable stages, including:

- Denial, refusing to believe that the event occurred
- Anger, realizing the magnitude of one's loss
- Bargaining, a fantasy stage whereby a person tries to bargain with God or with others to mitigate the impact of the trauma
- Depression, when the true impact of the loss sets in
- Acceptance, coming to terms with what has happened and getting on with life

However, the process of grieving is rarely so cut and dried or so linear, particularly among victims of trauma. The various stages might occur one after another, they might occur all at once, or they might jump back and forth. Some people may completely deny the impact of the event or even its reality. The thing is, with PTSD there is a tendency to get stuck, and these feelings can haunt you for weeks, months, or even years. The goal is to digest these intense emotions as best you can and move on to live your life more freely, without crippling obsessions.

What are some of the ways grief is manifest?

You may feel a depletion in energy, and you may even be literally unable to move around. You may feel depressed, and you may show little interest in the outside world, becoming obsessed or preoccupied with the loss or losses sustained. You may also experience a loss of appetite or an inability to sleep.

Are there any ways to deal with the pain of grief?

Yes. Although painful, understanding and experiencing grief as a process is essential for healing. However, there are things you can do to help yourself along the path. Firstly, recognize that all humans need to give themselves the space and the time to work through the process. If you can, take time off work. Although it is customary for places of employment to grant a certain amount of bereavement time, try to take more time if that is not sufficient. Most people are unable to function normally while they are grieving. Recognize the reality of what you have lost and understand that grieving is okay. Express your grief; talk about how you are feeling to a trusted friend, minister, counselor, or any other mental health professional. If talking is difficult, write about your feelings or draw them or find some other way to give vent to them. Some people even find it helpful to put together a symbolic memorial of their losses.

The bottom line, however, is to know that the people, things, or lost opportunities that you may be mourning were important enough to warrant these feelings you are experiencing. And remember, coming to terms with what one has lost does not mean pretending that it doesn't matter, it means realizing just how much it does matter but learning how to move on with your own life in spite of it.

I feel so helpless, like I can't do anything for myself anymore—things just seem to happen to me!

One of the things that makes a situation traumatic is the feeling of helplessness it provokes in its victims. The truth is, when this feeling occurs during the event, it is accurate and appropriate. You feel helpless because you *are* helpless. Once the event has passed, however, many victims continue to feel so helpless that they are unable to get on with their lives. They are often unable to complete the simple tasks of living that previously had never been a problem. According to Seligman, writing in 1975, a condition of learned helplessness exists. He demonstrated that in response to being exposed to a traumatic situation, organisms somehow adopt a certain passivity to their actions whereby they actually lose their motivation to respond when new stressful situations occur. Translated into human behavior, this might account for instances of revictimization, particularly among persons who remain in severely abusive relationships for long periods of time. Don't be angry with yourself for having these feelings of helplessness; they are symptoms of your condition.

Why do I feel so nervous, so jumpy and uneasy, like something bad is about to happen?

Anxiety is the commonly used term to describe an unpleasant state of tension that occurs in the body. In victims of trauma this feeling is precipitated by environmental triggers that set off a physiological response. Coping with intense feelings of anxiety is difficult to do on your own and usually needs therapeutic intervention or even medication.

I used to be a very religious person, but now I don't know what to believe.

It's not unusual for victims of trauma to lose or question their faith or belief systems, particularly if the abuse was inflicted by other humans or if several tragic circumstances have repeatedly struck you. How can you possibly begin to fathom how or why such a terrible thing could have happened? Traumatic events defy the very existence of a kind and just God, a kind and just society, or a kind and just world. Why did this happen to me? What is the reason for this? How can God do this to His people? These are some of the questions you may be asking yourself. Unfortunately, there are no answers for existential questions such as these, but feeling this way is a natural reaction to your suffering.

Incidents of trauma are usually random events. They are usually unexpected and strike out with power and violence. They can strike anyone at any time; the good, the bad, the rich, and the poor fall together. Your pleas for mercy go unanswered. Questioning your belief system is not a bad thing. It can lead to increased wisdom. For ultimately, as you begin to learn more about your condition and slowly start to recover, you will probably begin to change and grow in spiritual ways too.

I feel as though I have no future—that I'm going to die young or something!

Feelings of doom or of having a foreshortened future are characteristic feelings associated with PTSD. People who feel this way are unmotivated to do what it takes to get on with their lives. You may feel as though there really is no need to finish school, to be in a relationship, or to plan ahead in any other way. With treatment, though, these feelings will change.

Why do I feel so incapable and worthless?

Feeling worthless or inadequate stems from the low self-esteem brought about by the traumatic event itself. You may feel inadequate because you were rendered powerless and also as a result of secondary wounding. Symptoms of PTSD are also responsible for decreasing one's self-esteem, in that you feel bad about yourself because you are unable to predict or control your behavior.

I feel so depressed, life just doesn't seem worth living anymore!

Clinical depression and even thoughts of suicide can be directly related to the untreated symptoms of trauma. Symptoms of depression are extremely debilitating and, unlike "the blues," which all of us suffer from time to time, get worse and not better over time. Symptoms of clinical depression include weight loss or gain, recurrent sleep disorders, severe fatigue, poor concentration, little or no interest in daily activities (including those activities that previously gave you pleasure), very low self-esteem, excessive feelings of inappropriate guilt, and ongoing thoughts of death or suicide.

How can I make these feelings go away?

If you are experiencing four or more of the above symptoms to the extent that you are unable to function normally in everyday life, you probably are suffering from clinical depression and need to secure the help of a trained mental health professional. Psychotherapy and medication are both useful and popular forms of treatment for depression, but although they may ease the symptoms, if your depression was caused by trauma, just treating the symptoms of depression will most likely be insufficient.

Is it possible not to know what I'm feeling?

Yes. This too is not uncommon. Being out of touch with your feelings or unable to identify them in words is often more of a manifestation of your specific upbringing than a result of your traumatic experience. Some people grow up in families or in cultures where expression of feelings is frowned upon; this is especially common among men who learn from a very early age that expressing one's feelings is a sign of weakness. For people with this type of background, it is quite possible that being able to identify specific feelings can be a problem. Some victims, however, may find that they simply do not have the words in their vocabulary to describe the magnitude of their feelings. Creative arts therapies are especially useful when this is the case (see chapter 7).

References

Flannery, R. *Post-Traumatic Stress Disorder: The Victim's Guide to Healing and Recovery*. New York: Crossroad Publishing Company, 1992.

Matsakis, A. *I Can't Get Over It: A Handbook for Trauma Survivors*. Oakland, Calif.: New Harbinger Publications, 1994.

Herman, J. *Trauma and Recovery*. New York: Basic Books, 1997.

Kubler-Ross, E. *On Death and Dying*. New York, Collier Books, 1997.

Matsakis, A. *Post-Traumatic Stress Disorder: A Complete Treatment Guide*. Oakland, Calif.: New Harbinger Publications, 1994.

Chapter 5
WHAT CAUSES PTSD?

Post-traumatic stress disorder occurs when a trauma overwhelms the mind's defenses. After the mind is overwhelmed, it changes in certain characteristic ways. These changes can be measured by brain scans, by measurement of body chemicals, and by clinical observation. In this chapter we will try to explain the current thinking about the development of this disorder. We'll start by looking at PTSD from a "brain" or biological perspective and then look at it from a "mind" or psychological perspective. While details remain to be worked out, researchers are getting closer to more fully understanding PTSD and how it affects both our brains and our minds. We'll start by looking at how the brain is changed in PTSD.

So trauma actually changes my brain?

Before we go into details about PTSD, you should realize that our brains (and bodies) are responding to the environment every second of every day, whether we are asleep or awake. That is what brains do: they help us adapt to the ever-changing world. If we're asleep, our minds may seem to be resting, but the brain is still performing vital functions like breathing, maintenance of muscle tone, and dreaming. If we're awake, our minds need to keep track of dozens of tasks, only a few of which we may be aware of at any one time. And there are plenty of times during a typical day that we may be conscious of nothing much in particular, but we still remember to turn off the lights, answer the telephone, and smile at the appropriate moment. To keep up with all of this, our brains are constantly changing in subtle, interesting ways. You may have seen pictures of a brain, and it might look like a solid object, but it is actually a fantastically sensitive organ. Many researchers consider the human brain to be the most complex thing on earth. And, given all the things it has to keep up with, our brains work wonderfully well.

What happens when the brain is stressed?

When we are confronted with danger, our brains and bodies jump into overdrive. For example, if you are taking a hike, you may feel relaxed and happy and be aware of the birds, the trees, and a recipe for that night's dinner. If you suddenly see a bear fifty feet down the trail, you'd tend to stop thinking of the birds, trees, and recipe, and begin to assess the danger. Is this the kind of bear that might attack? Should you run away? Should you stand perfectly still and hope the bear walks away? Should you throw a rock at the bear? Not recommended, by the way. The ability of your mind to think will be determined by several factors. If you live near the woods and have often seen this bear, you will probably stay perfectly relaxed and may feel pleased to see an old friend. If you've never seen a wild bear before, you might have a typical stress reaction, which we'll discuss in a minute. If you were once mauled by a wild animal, and you have PTSD, your reaction will most likely be typical of someone with PTSD and will be different from the average person who has a typical stress reaction.

What's a typical stress reaction?

Let's continue with the example of the bear. If you are the average person and you see a bear fifty feet away, you will concentrate your attention on that threat. Your arms and legs will tighten and be ready to spring into action. You won't waste energy thinking about the recipe for dinner, since if you don't properly assess the threat, you might not be around for dinner! Similarly, your body won't devote energy to digesting your lunch or to feeling minor pain or to any other nonessential task. The body's attention is devoted entirely to the bear. People have been reacting this way to stress since the dawn of time. For the past eighty-five years, it's been called the "fight-or-flight" response.

What does "fight or flight" mean?

It means that when we are confronted with a threat, we tend to respond by fighting or fleeing. A third option has recently been added to the list: freezing. Some might say that freezing is similar to fleeing, in that both imply a certain amount of passivity. All three survival techniques are important parts of our defense system, and we all learn to use each of them.

Is it possible to measure this fight-or-flight response?

Yes. Modern technology has developed a variety of ways to look at our responses. Let's take a look at some of the immediate changes that are caused by stress. This will help us when we try to make sense of the PTSD response.

When we say that our bodies tense, we mean that our muscles tense. In order for our muscles to tense, they need a greater amount of food and oxygen. Muscles get their food from sugar and get their oxygen from blood cells. In order for muscles to get their nutrients, then, they have to get more of a blood supply. Two immediate ways to increase blood flow are to in-

crease the heart rate and to increase the blood pressure.
And if we see a bear, we feel exactly these changes: Our
muscles tense and our heart begins to pound. At the
same time, a whole series of other reactions will take
place: We breathe faster so that our oxygen use is increased; our pupils dilate so we can see more clearly;
and the blood flow to the brain increases, which sharp-
ens our thinking. For our bodies to perform at their
peak capacities, as they might need to with the bear,
these coordinated responses have to take place.

**How does the body know to do things like increase the
heart rate and blood pressure?**

When we perceive a threat, our brain immediately releases chemicals called neuropeptides. These neuropeptides lead to a bunch of characteristic responses,
including the changes in heart rate and blood pressure.
These neuropeptides have names like dopamine, adrenaline, and noradrenaline. For the purposes of this book
these names aren't important. The important thing to
remember is something we all know firsthand: when
we're confronted by a threat to our safety, we experience a fight-or-flight reaction.

**Let's say we run back to our nearby car and roll up the
windows. The bear is nowhere in sight. What happens
then?**

For most people, when we reach safety, we feel safe.
Our heart stops racing and pounding. We might feel
pain that we'd previously ignored. We might need to go
to the bathroom. Our breathing slows. We might close
our eyes. We're home free.

**What happens to all those fight-or-flight neuropep-
tides? Shouldn't we keep feeling stressed until they get
digested or worn out or something?**

This is an important piece of the PTSD puzzle. At the very same time that the body is releasing the neuropeptides that cause the fight-or-flight response, the body is also releasing neuropeptides that tell the adrenal cortex to produce cortisol. One of cortisol's many responsibilities is to shut down the stress response when the threat has disappeared. This type of automatic regulatory system is absolutely critical to the functioning of our brains and bodies.

How does all this relate to PTSD?

In PTSD, people have experienced a trauma, or, more commonly, a series of traumas, that have overwhelmed the system. Their regulatory system doesn't work normally. They don't shut down their stress response. They continue to feel a threat when the threat is nowhere in sight.

So you're saying that PTSD develops when the body doesn't produce enough cortisol after a trauma?

There's more to the story than that, but cortisol does seem to be an important factor in the development of PTSD. For example, researchers studied the cortisol levels of people who had been brought to the emergency room after having been involved in serious automobile accidents. They waited six months and then interviewed the people who'd been in the accidents. The ones who went on to develop PTSD had low cortisol levels immediately after their accidents. Interestingly, the ones who went on to develop serious depression (but not PTSD) had high cortisol levels. People who did not have serious psychological problems after their accidents had cortisol levels that fell between those two groups. Similar results have been found in soldiers while they were on duty in Vietnam and in women after they've been raped.

So people with PTSD respond to trauma differently. Is that what causes PTSD in the first place?

That isn't certain, but it does seem that some people become so overwhelmed by their trauma that they become unable to regulate this stress response system. Their cortisol levels are unable to inhibit the intensity of their fight-or-flight response, and they constantly feel like their lives are threatened. A seemingly small reminder can, therefore, send people with PTSD into what feels like an uncontrolled tailspin.

So everything is related to cortisol?

The situation is more complicated than that. We've talked about how there are three cardinal symptoms of PTSD. One is increased arousal, and that does seem to be quite connected to this neuropeptide-cortisol system. In addition, these particular neuropeptides are related to a whole host of symptoms connected to PTSD, such as depression, rage, and mood swings. Another cardinal symptom relates to numbing, and numbing seems to be related to a different system.

Where does numbing come in?

Stress causes the release of natural opiates that act as natural painkillers. In the example of the bear, if we have to run through the forest, we probably won't feel cuts or bruises until we make it safely to the car. In addition, we may not feel much fear or anxiety while we are in the middle of the crisis. These natural opiates are protective and normal.

How do the natural opiates cause a problem?

It is useful to become partially anesthetized during a severe threat. Natural opiates can, however, become too much of a good thing. As with the energizing neuropeptides we talked about earlier, natural opiates can get stuck in the "on" position. PTSD can partly be seen as a state of alternating between numbness and overarousal, and these systems are significantly at fault.

Do these natural opiates have anything to do with prescription painkillers?

Yes. One study of combat veterans showed that fifteen minutes of watching battle scenes from the movie *Platoon* led to a reduction of pain sensitivity equivalent to eight milligrams of morphine.

If everybody gets stressed at times, why are some people unable to just get past it?

While all of our understanding is tentative at this point, in some ways, PTSD seems to have something to do with memory. The trauma can become imprinted in our brains partly because of the overwhelming intensity of the stress. Numbness from the natural opiates seems to reduce the ability to process and digest the traumatic experience. It seems that unusually high or low levels of cortisol can affect memory. There are many contributing factors, but it does seem that one vital aspect to the predisposing experience is a sense of futility. The person who goes on to develop PTSD has generally been exposed to a severe trauma in which the fight-or-flight response didn't work. The numbing response didn't work. Nothing worked. And this overwhelming experience derails the brain's stress response system.

What parts of the brain are most affected in PTSD?

Apparently, a major culprit in PTSD is the interaction between the limbic system and part of the frontal cortex. We won't go into detail, but the limbic system sits in the middle of the brain and is heavily involved in memory and feelings. The frontal lobe lies behind your forehead and is responsible for much of your ability to think and process information. It seems that two things go wrong in the limbic system in PTSD. The first is that part of the limbic system (called the amygdala) becomes overly sensitive to threats. A second part of the limbic system (the hippocampus) is supposed to put the possible threat into context and, if the threat is no big deal, help you relax. In PTSD these parts of the limbic system seem to get out of whack.

The frontal lobe is the part of the brain that is supposed to act as a "governor" of these systems. In PTSD the frontal lobe loses some of its connection to the limbic system, and the intense feelings generated within the limbic system seem to take on a life of their own. The frontal lobe becomes unable to process and digest the threat and help extinguish the anxiety. This can lead to overarousal and repetition of the trauma, for example.

What does all this have to do with the neuropeptides that you were talking about?

The neuropeptides are the messengers between these different systems.

Why should I learn anything about neurology? How can this information help me?

There are two reasons to learn it. First, such knowledge can help reduce the helplessness that comes from having a confusing set of symptoms. The second is that this explanation can be a useful metaphor for your experience and your recovery. Many people describe the intense anxiety of PTSD as being beyond their control, for example. When we talk about things being within our mental control, we are generally talking about the thinking that is done within the frontal lobe. This model fits that experience: The memories and feelings within the limbic system are indeed out of kilter and cut off from the thinking part of the brain, the frontal lobe. As far as recovery is concerned, it becomes vital to learn techniques to calm yourself when you feel threatened and anxious. In addition, it is important to develop ways to process the threatening information and put the anxiety to rest.

These explanations make a certain amount of sense, but they remind me of a biologist trying to explain crying. He can describe the process physiologically, but I'm more interested in the meaning of the tears. Is there a theory of PTSD that doesn't include talk about neuropeptides and the limbic system?

Sure, though it should be noted that even psychoanalysts have become more interested in the neurobiology of feelings and behavior in the past twenty years. And a goal of any good psychological theory is for the biology to fit with our personal experience. Having said that, there are a number of interesting thoughts about PTSD that make no mention of biology. The first is a fairly typical psychodynamic or psychoanalytic view of PTSD:

As we grow up, we develop relationships with other people, become more aware of our inner lives, learn to master our environments, and gradually develop a core sense of ourselves and the world in which we live. These are not easy tasks, and all of us face many adversities as we age. In fact, we all need a certain amount of adversity and stress if we are to grow into mature, flexible people. Conflict and stress are part of the very fabric of being human, and we all learn—more or less—how to deal with these problems.

People who develop PTSD have been confronted

with a trauma that has overwhelmed them. It may be a single trauma or a repeated trauma or a prolonged trauma. It might be a trauma from childhood or one that strikes them in old age. There are a variety of thoughts for each type of trauma, but suffice it to say that the meaning of the trauma has been overwhelming, that their place in the world has been shaken. Any or all of their core belief systems may have failed them, whether the belief is in themselves, in their environment, or in other people. This devastation has affected their ability to think clearly about issues related to the trauma, and it has affected their ability to realistically assess their own feelings. Intensely painful memories are followed by periods of numbing. These may be efforts at making sense of the trauma, but by themselves these feelings don't seem to get anywhere. While people with PTSD may have significant areas of psychological health, the post-traumatic stress disorder has wounded them in a very personal way. Successful treatment would need to address each of these concerns.

Does this theory conflict with the biological theory?

These theories remain controversial and are in some flux, but they don't need to contradict one another. As we've said, a good psychological theory should make biological sense. For example, the psychological theory describes a decreased ability to think and make sense of feelings. Modern brain scans of people with PTSD have demonstrated a problem in the parts of the brain devoted to thinking and feeling. Similarly, measurements of chemicals have demonstrated problems in the metabolism of neuropeptides that control mood, impulsivity, and anger.

What would be another psychological theory?

A second type of psychological theory is more behavioral, though it does overlap with the psychodynamic theory and the biological theory. A "behavioral" explanation tends to avoid the issue of ultimate causes but instead focuses on the observable fact that traumatic memories are very painful. People tend to push away those painful memories and feelings. Unfortunately, the trauma does not disappear but comes back in the form of flashbacks, nightmares, and phobias. Because they are not properly digested, these painful feelings and memories keep coming back and tend to take on a life of their own. This would lead to PTSD.

These theories make PTSD sound hard to treat. Is there a way to get better?

There are several types of treatments that have been very useful for people with PTSD. They are outlined in the next two chapters.

References

Bourne, P. B., R. M. Rose, and J. W. Mason. "17-OHCS Levels in Combat: Special Forces 'A' Team Under Threat of Attack." *Archives General Psychiatry* 19, 1968, pp. 135–140.

Butler, K. "The Biology of Fear." *The Family Therapy Networker,* July/August 1996, p. 25.

Cannon, W. B. "Emergency Function of Adrenal Medulla in Pain and Major Emotions." *American Journal of Physiology* 1914(3), pp. 356–372.

McFarlane, A. C., M. Atchison, and R. Yehuda. "The Acute Stress Response Following Motor Vehicle Accidents and Its Relation to PTSD". In: R. Yehuda and A. C. McFarlane, eds., *Psychobiology of Post-Traumatic Stress Disorder.* New York: New York Academy of Sciences, 1997, pp. 437–439.

Rauch, S. L., L. M. Shin, P. J. Whalen, et al. "Neuroimaging and the Neuroanatomy of Posttraumatic Stress Disorder." *CNS Spectrums* 3:7, pp. 31–41.

Resnick, H. S., R. Yehuda, R. K. Pitman, et al. "Effect of Previous Trauma on Acute Plasma Cortisol Level Following Rape." *American Journal of Psychiatry* 152, 1995, pp. 1675–1677.

Chapter 6
FINDING HELP

I think I have PTSD and need help. What do I do now?

The recognition that you have a problem is often the most important step in the recovery process. You might want to take a little time just to let the idea sink in. Give yourself some credit for getting to this point before you try to fix things. You have probably spent time working to make your life better, but you may not have realized that you had a specific problem that should be labeled PTSD. Maybe you hadn't been aware that other people feel the same way you do. Maybe you've been struggling with symptoms related to PTSD for many years. Maybe you've developed other problems in addition to PTSD.

Your job at this point is to explore a variety of options. There is a very good chance that the possibility of treatment makes you nervous. You might want to take some deep breaths and try to get comfortable. Learning to feel safe may be the most important skill that you need.

Whenever I try to get help, I immediately feel worse. What should I do?

One of the most treacherous aspects of PTSD is that treatment often does make people feel worse. Any reminder of the trauma can cause intense anxiety, which is the reason that you've probably learned ways to avoid these reminders. Treatment usually consists of some recollection, and so treatment can traumatize you all over again. It becomes important, therefore, to learn how to approach the trauma in a safe and manageable way. It may be necessary, for example, to learn some relaxation and breathing techniques before the trauma can even be addressed.

My family says that I need to see somebody right away, that I've wasted too much time already. Are they over-reacting?

This is difficult to say. PTSD can be life threatening. If you are suicidal or homicidal, for example, hospitalization may even be necessary. Your family may also be concerned that without help your symptoms could get worse. This too is a realistic concern. But you cannot be helped unless you feel ready to take the necessary steps yourself.

Who will be able to help me?

Your options are plentiful. Possibilities include psychiatrists, psychologists, social workers, social service workers, community service workers, emergency service personnel, family members, and even your friends.

How do you tell the difference between a psychiatrist, a psychologist, a social worker, and an analyst?

Psychiatrists have gone to medical school and then have done at least four years of specialty training in psychiatry. Because they are physicians, psychiatrists are the only therapists who can prescribe medications. In addition, if you need hospitalization, you should know that psychiatrists generally control hospital admissions. Psychiatrists also tend to be the most expensive kind of therapists, although most insurance companies do cover part of the cost. Some psychiatrists primarily do psychotherapy, while others do a bit of therapy but focus largely on medication treatments. You may be referred to a medicating psychiatrist if your primary therapist is a social worker or a psychologist and medication is something you need.

Psychologists have earned either a master's degree (M.A.) or a doctorate (Ph.D.) in psychology. Social workers have earned a degree in social work. A social worker might be a L.C.S.W. (a licensed clinical social worker) or an M.S.W. (master of social work) or have a Ph.D. in social work. As with psychiatrists, insurance often covers part of the treatment. A person who has completed training in any of these fields has had a significant amount of clinical experience under supervision.

A psychoanalyst is a psychiatrist, psychologist, or social worker who has taken additional training in psychoanalysis. Psychoanalytic training can take up to ten additional years for the therapist, which ensures a greater baseline level of clinical experience. This training does not ensure experience with PTSD or competence in other forms of treatment, such as cognitive-behavioral therapy.

It is important to know that anyone can call themselves a therapist and set up a practice, even without having a license. Although unlicensed therapists may be quite empathetic and kindly, and you may be tempted to see one for treatment, don't do it. The licensing process ensures a baseline level of experience, and you should try to get the very best help you can.

I don't think I'm ready to see a therapist. Are there other options?

One of the major goals of PTSD treatment is for you to gain a sense of control over your life. Your treatment is a good time to start gaining this sense of control. Approach your recovery as you see fit. For example, Jessica had never had a gynecological exam despite the fact that she was twenty-seven years old. She was terrified at the idea, just as she was terrified of many other things, and she knew that her fear was related to having been raped when she was ten. She decided to go and see a gynecologist who had a special interest in such issues. Jessica was especially concerned that the rape had somehow damaged her, that her genitals had been ruined in some way. In Jessica's case a gynecological exam was helpful in that it convinced her that she was physically normal, and it proved to be the first step into a deeper exploration of her fearfulness.

Anthony had also been abused as a child, and he found that reading about the subject led him to attend a couple of lectures, which led him to a support group, which then led him into individual therapy. He experienced a dramatic improvement in his PTSD symptoms.

Amber had been in therapy for years and had been able to discuss a whole variety of issues with her therapist. Neither she nor her therapist had ever conceptualized her issues as related to PTSD. When they did recognize that her constellation of problems were consistent with PTSD, they were able to focus the treatment far more effectively.

There are many ways to pursue treatment. Your job is to find the set of approaches that works for you.

I'm afraid of doctors and therapists. Is there anyone else who can help me?

Yes, you can receive counseling, which differs from therapy in that its purpose is to educate and to advise rather than to focus on your specific feelings and behavior. This form of treatment is offered by social service organizations such as rape crisis centers, Veteran's Administration hospitals, and centers for battered women. Counselors are generally well trained and experienced, although they generally haven't received as much training as a psychiatrist, a psychologist, or a social worker.

How do I go about finding a therapist?

There is no one way to find a therapist. You may want to ask your friends or your physician for a referral. They know you and may have some good suggestions. Your local hospital probably has a referral system and may be able to steer you toward those people who are experts in the field. Depending on the size of your community, you may find an appropriate support group by looking in the telephone book or on the Internet. You will also find a selection of useful resources and organizations that can help you at the back of this book.

As previously discussed, people with PTSD get very upset when anything reminds them of their trauma. For this reason, asking for help may be painful. Be aware of this and try to make yourself as safe and as comfortable as possible when talking about your feelings.

Once you have compiled a list of possible resources, you will need to screen them to find out about such things as expense, location, and availability. You should also feel free to ask prospective therapists about their training and experience, especially with regard to PTSD. Many practicing therapists are very good in their particular areas but have minimal experience in dealing with the victims of trauma. An ethical therapist will tell you if he or she doesn't often treat people with your problems.

Should I interview several therapists or try to work with the first one?

This is a personal decision. Some people suggest interviewing several therapists prior to making a decision. If you feel comfortable with the first therapist you find, however, it's fine to go ahead and work with that person.

Which is better, a male therapist or a female therapist?

There is no right or wrong answer to this question. Some people feel that a female therapist may better understand some of the things women go through in our society and that this can be useful in situations of rape or sexual abuse. However, this is not necessarily the rule. The most essential element to recovery is a sound working relationship between therapist and client, so whether you decide to go with a male or female, you need to feel comfortable and secure with the person with whom you commit yourself to work.

I was sexually abused as a child and am worried that a male therapist might try to force me to have sex with him. Isn't it better for me to see a woman?

A therapist who forces you to have sex with him is a rapist. This is illegal and rare.

I'm in treatment now. My problem is that I want to date my psychiatrist and he's refusing. I think we should stop treatment and get a female therapist so that he and I could go out. He says my feelings are part of the treatment process and that they relate to my having been abused as a child. What does he mean?

It is very common for people who have been abused as children to go into treatment and then develop erotic feelings for their therapist. The drive to act on these feelings may feel intense. One goal of your treatment will be to better understand your desire to step over boundaries, and your therapist is doing the right thing by staying on the ethical side of the line. You should also know that it is malpractice for your psychiatrist to have a sexual relationship with you, even if you do end treatment. The view is, "Once a patient, always a patient."

Will it help to see a therapist who has more in common with me?

A lot of people seek out therapists who seem to have something in common with them. The link could be gender or it could be religion, age, sexual orientation, military background, ethnicity, or anything you can notice. If such a link makes you more comfortable, that's fine. In the real world most people do fine with most well-trained therapists.

Will I need to stay with the therapist once I have made a commitment?

No, you never need to stick with a therapist, but once you have made a commitment, give it a fair try. Healing from trauma is often slow and painful. Difficulties may be due to the treatment process itself rather than the therapist. As we've discussed, even mentioning your trauma might be painful and retraumatizing. If you are especially anxious about a long-term commitment, you might suggest a six-week trial period to see if the two of you get along.

I've tried therapy before, and it was okay for a while but then it fell apart. I just didn't feel as though I was getting any better. Why should I try again?

You should try to figure out why the therapy didn't work. Maybe your first therapist focused primarily on discussing the meaning of your trauma when you needed a more cognitive-behavioral approach. Or maybe the reverse was true, that your therapist focused on goals and tasks and homework (using a cognitive-behavioral approach) when you needed someone to empathetically witness your difficulties. It could be that you just didn't have a good fit with your first (or second) therapist. Therapy can be hard work and you need to be highly motivated to change. Maybe you weren't particularly committed to change in the past. PTSD treatment can be painful because it generally requires some reworking of your traumatic memories. It may be easier to live with your symptoms than to work through your problems with your therapist. There are many reasons why your therapy may have fallen apart, but this does not mean that it will never work for you.

If you are currently in therapy and feel misunderstood or frustrated, it can be a great opportunity for you to work on your communication skills and try to express your feelings. People with PTSD have a tendency to feel misunderstood and criticized. An important part of your therapy is learning to try new ways of relating. Tell your therapist the ways in which you are unhappy. You might be surprised at what happens.

I intend to see a therapist someday, but right now my life feels out of control. Shouldn't I wait and go into therapy when I get more organized?

You should go to a therapist when you feel like changing, no matter how messy you feel your life is. Therapists assume that things in your life are rocky or you wouldn't be calling in the first place.

Will my therapist take my health insurance?

This is something you need to ask during the initial screening process. Most insurance companies include mental health as part of their treatment plans, although the extent of coverage varies and is generally not as comprehensive as coverage for nonpsychiatric illnesses.

Individual therapists and clinics will often reduce the standard fee if necessary. In addition, most support groups operate free of charge, as do Twelve-Step programs such as Alcoholics Anonymous.

Will I need to have a physical examination?

It may or may not be necessary to get a physical examination. If you've been physically assaulted or raped, for example, you should get a physical examination done immediately. Similarly, if your trauma involved some sort of personal illness, your physical well-being should be closely followed. Feeling better physically can help you feel better mentally. In addition, there are some physical illnesses that cause anxiety and depression. A thorough physical examination can help pinpoint what is ailing you.

Is there a blood test for PTSD?

No, there are no blood tests to diagnose PTSD. Some physical problems can mimic some PTSD symptoms, so your doctor may want to do some blood tests to rule out those conditions as being the source of your problems. For example, thyroid disease can cause depression and anxiety and so thyroid function tests may be necessary. PTSD is a diagnosis determined by clinical symptoms.

I have a problem with alcohol and drugs, but I view PTSD as my primary problem. Will a therapist agree to see me?

Some will, but the general feeling is that progress with your PTSD will be almost impossible while you are actively abusing drugs and alcohol. It doesn't matter if the substance abuse was caused by the PTSD or vise versa. Mood-altering substances may feel like your only hope against the symptoms of PTSD, but these substances make it almost impossible to address the symptoms and dissipate their force. You should strongly consider a drug rehabilitation program or a Twelve-Step program.

What are Twelve-Step programs?

Alcoholics Anonymous (AA) and Narcotics Anonymous (NA) are two very well established programs designed to help their members achieve lasting sobriety. Based on a set of twelve carefully structured steps, members are encouraged to see their addiction as a disease over which they have no control, to relinquish their addiction to a higher power, and to regain control over their lives by taking sobriety one day at a time. These groups are found all over the world and require nothing from their members except a desire to become sober. The atmosphere is caring and supportive. Other Twelve-Step programs include Overeaters Anonymous (OA) for people with eating disorders, Gamblers Anonymous (GA) for compulsive gamblers, and Debtor's Anonymous (DA) for overspenders. Remember, these are all conditions that can be associated with trauma.

Twelve-Step programs are by far the most popular way for people to get help with their addictions. Some people, however, object to the spiritual nature of such programs. If that's the case, you might try organizations such as Rational Recovery (RR) or SMART.

How does Rational Recovery (RR) differ from AA?

RR is not a support group. It is an organization that has developed a set of instructions on how to quit an addiction. Participants in the program are taught that their addictions are not a disease but the result of an addictive voice in their heads enticing them to imbibe. The method taught by RR is called AVRT (Addictive

Voice Recognition Technique) and is a rapid deprogramming technique. Participants learn how to recognize their addictive voice and how to control it. Participants in the program are also encouraged not to use the program as a support group but rather to learn the technique and then to implement it themselves. The feeling is that it is healthier not to continually mingle with others who feel insecure about their own sobriety.

What is SMART?

SMART (Self-Management And Recovery Training) is a not-for-profit organization that provides self-help and support for people who have problems in their lives as a result of their addictions. Although its primary focus is addiction, SMART can be used to address numerous other problems associated with daily living, including stress, anger, anxiety, and even depression. Participants form small discussion groups and are taught a variety of self-management techniques, following methods derived from cognitive-behavioral therapies. SMART differs from AA because addictions are not seen as a disease, but rather as a bad habit that can be changed.

Is it true that medication may help with my PTSD?

This is a difficult question to answer, and there is certainly no right answer for everyone. Medications are sometimes used to diminish symptoms that are directly related to PTSD, such as anxiety. In addition, PTSD often exists alongside another major illness such as major depression, and medications are frequently used to treat the coexisting depression. There are also medications that seem to work directly on some of the hallmark symptoms of PTSD, like increased arousal. There is a lot of research being conducted in this area, and recommendations may change in the future. This subject will be discussed in greater depth in another chapter.

So is it possible to get better just by taking a pill?

Some people with PTSD do improve on medication alone. For the vast majority of people, however, medication works best when combined with some form of talk therapy.

If it is possible to get better just by taking medication, couldn't I just go to my regular doctor and get a prescription?

It may be tempting to try to see your problems as purely physical and get some medication from your internist or gynecologist. In fact, your doctor may go along with your request. Nevertheless, you should be evaluated and treated by someone who has a lot of experience with your disorder and a lot of experience with psychiatric medication. Not only will this improve the likelihood that you'll get better, but a psychiatrist is better able to minimize possible side effects from the medication.

I feel nervous about taking medication. How can I be sure it's going to work?

Before you take any medication, feel free to discuss your symptoms with your psychiatrist and ask as many questions as you want. Ask about the types of medications that can be used to treat your specific problem, and find out about their benefits and side effects and how long it will take before they start to work. Medication needs to be closely monitored to ensure that it is working correctly and that you are taking the appropriate dose. Together with your psychiatrist you will determine whether the medication is having the desired results, whether the dosage needs to be tweaked, or whether a different drug needs to be administered.

Is hospitalization ever necessary?

Treatment of PTSD is usually done outside of a hospital, but there are three main reasons why being admitted into a hospital may be necessary. First, you may need to be hospitalized if you are suicidal or homicidal, so that the hospital's structure and safety can allow you to get effective treatment and recompose yourself. Second, if you are addicted to alcohol or drugs, you may need to go into a hospital for detoxification. When the body has become dependent on alcohol or drugs, breaking the habit can be difficult, especially for the first couple of days, when the body goes through physical withdrawal—headaches, vomiting, seizures, tremor, and delusions can all occur. Hospitals can help you safely through this period. Finally, there have been efforts to use hospitals to treat specialized groups such as Vietnam veterans and child abuse victims. These attempts have met with mixed results and are now somewhat unusual. As we've repeatedly stressed, your own treatment should be tailored to your own needs.

What does therapy hope to achieve?

The primary objective of any therapy is to help you feel better about yourself and to help you regain control over the aspects of your life that have become unmanageable. With regard to the treatment of PTSD, therapy should also try to achieve the following objectives:

- to develop a greater sense of safety
- to help you identify the traumatic event or events that precipitated your symptoms
- to help educate you as to the nature of your condi-

tion, including how or why your symptoms occurred
- to suggest ways to help you find relief from your
symptoms
- to help you receive any treatment you may need for
coexisting conditions such as substance abuse or
eating disorders
- to help you become realistic regarding your perceptions of danger and to help you secure a safe environment when you need one
- to help you tolerate intimacy and develop a deeper
sense of trust

Is there anything in particular that I should expect from my therapist?

Regardless of the type of treatment for your PTSD,
your therapist should try to create a situation of safety
and trust. This may not be easy, but it is critical to your
recovery. It would be unusual if you felt truly safe at
the beginning of any psychological treatment, especially if you suffer from PTSD. This is one of the most
difficult aspects of PTSD therapy. The exact people
who need to trust somebody in order for the treatment
to work are often the exact people who don't easily
trust. This mistrust may be obvious, as in Bill's case.
Bill had tried treatment a number of times since he
returned from Vietnam, where he had been held captive
as a POW. During his most recent consultation he
loudly described never having been satisfied by any
doctor, clinic, or therapist in his life. He felt that he
was being used as a guinea pig by researchers and as a
cash cow by therapists in private practice. With someone like Bill it might be necessary from the very beginning to make him aware that his sense of trust had
probably been crushed by his POW experience and that

quite possibly his mistrust would enter into any treatment he attempted. Instead of using his fear and mistrust as a sign that it was time for therapy to end, the therapist might point out that his feelings of mistrust were, rather, an indication that the therapy had begun.

With Annie the situation was different. Having suffered a childhood of abuse, Annie had spent her whole life as a seemingly compliant, friendly, and trusting person. Underneath her pleasant attitude, she was disconnected, angry, and scared. She hated having those "bad" feelings, and when they began to well to the surface, she tended to end all relationships. In cases such as hers the development of a therapeutic relationship will cause those negative feelings to emerge, and it will take a lot of work on her and her therapist's part to strengthen her feelings of safety and trust.

It is often difficult to learn to trust and feel safe again. However, don't forget that every single treatment must work with these issues to enable you to escape the limiting consequences of your PTSD. Only then can you develop a treatment plan.

What is a treatment plan?

Many therapists will want to help you structure a treatment plan for your recovery. As the name implies, a treatment plan is a course of action that might outline specific therapeutic goals and ways of obtaining them. One of the real advantages of a treatment plan is that it might help you feel more grounded and clearer about your treatment. Treatment plans should be flexible, capable of being adjusted regularly to suit your changing needs as you begin to heal.

Why do I need to be involved in developing a treatment plan? I'm not a therapist, and if I knew what to do, I wouldn't be seeing one.

Suggesting that you be instrumental in designing your own treatment plan does not mean that you are expected to know exactly what to do. However, your input is essential in determining the course of action. When trauma strikes, it usually renders its victims powerless, and it is these feelings of powerlessness that linger on, long after the event has passed. By actively participating in your treatment, you will start to redevelop your sense of control over your own life—a feeling destroyed by the trauma. Active participation in your treatment is a first step to regaining control over your life.

Are there any priorities that must be considered in the development of a treatment plan?

There may be. The first is to secure immediate safety. If you are currently in an abusive or otherwise dangerous situation, you need to find a place of safety. If you require immediate medical attention, you need to seek medical help. In addition, if you have a substance abuse problem or a coexisting psychiatric problem, such as depression, it will probably be necessary to address these problems before a treatment for PTSD will be effective.

How long will treatment take?

Treatment time varies a great deal. If you experienced a natural disaster that destroyed your home, for example, and you developed a relatively mild case of PTSD, focused treatment may be rapidly successful. If, however, your trauma was especially severe and/or long-lasting, and if it occurred during a time when you were particularly vulnerable (such as childhood), recovery will probably take a lot longer. And for a certain percentage of people the troublesome symptoms of PTSD

are never entirely eliminated, regardless of treatment.
For such people, recovery can be a lifelong process.

**I know I need help, but I don't feel comfortable with
the idea of securing help from a complete stranger. Do
I have any other options?**

Your most valuable source of help may be right under
your nose—that is, your family and friends. These people love and care about you and generally (if your family is relatively strong and intact) have your best
interests at heart. Healthy families are generally good
at solving problems. During a time of crisis, members
often bond together, pooling ideas and resources to
help you cope with your crisis. They may be able to
provide emotional and/or financial support and come
up with all kinds of creative ways to help you get back
on your feet.

**What if the trauma is being caused by a family mem-
ber?**

If this is the case, securing help from someone outside
of the family is your best bet.

**My sister has had PTSD for the past year. I feel bad
about complaining, but she's almost impossible to live
with. What can I do?**

Living with a person who has PTSD may become extremely difficult and disruptive. For her sake, and for
yours, it may be necessary to receive family therapy.
For example, trauma survivors often react to stress
with angry outbursts or cold withdrawal. This can create tension and fear in family members, which makes
them miserable, and also can cause the trauma survivor
to feel even more misunderstood and alone. Therapy

can teach both of you how to interact with each other in a better, more productive manner.

What is family therapy?

In family therapy, the whole family is seen together by the therapist. The focus is on the family as an interactive system rather than on any one particular person. In the case of PTSD, family therapy can be used to educate the family about the nature of PTSD and the symptoms experienced by the afflicted family member.

My family doesn't want to attend family sessions. I think it's because they're afraid of talking about family secrets. How do I get them interested?

Many families have secrets of one kind or another. Alcoholism and drug abuse are common secrets, as are physical and sexual abuse. These issues almost always have a serious impact and are sometimes the reason why you are seeking treatment in the first place. It may be necessary perhaps to hold sessions without all the family members at once, or it may be necessary for family members to talk individually to the therapist prior to the onset of family therapy. In some instances it may be necessary to forgo family therapy altogether. In general, though, families tend to want to participate once they realize that their involvement can be useful.

I've been in therapy for some time and I know that I'm getting better. My relationship with my husband, however, seems to be falling apart. How can this be?

As people with PTSD start getting well, their loved ones have to learn to adapt to the change. And adapting to change, even if the change is for the better, is not always easy. For example, as Annie recovered from her PTSD, she became more outgoing and sociable. She met some new friends and started going to the gym after work and playing cards two evenings a week. Her husband was pleased and proud initially, but then he began to resent the fact that she was busier than she had ever been before. Without being fully aware of it, he became jealous of her new friends and irritated that he had to cook for himself while she was out playing cards. Then, as she became more sociable, he began to wonder if she was having an affair. As he became more angry and judgmental Annie began to wonder whether their marriage was such a good idea. They sought marriage counseling, in which he was able to talk about his insecurities and she was able to talk about her need to spread her wings a little. By developing an increased understanding of her recovery process, he was able to feel less jealous and she began to feel less boxed in. Their marriage ended up stronger than it had ever been.

What happens if I don't get treatment?

You may get better on your own, especially if you experienced only one trauma and your symptoms are relatively mild. For most people, PTSD has a strong tendency to stick if it isn't aggressively treated. And if left untreated, it may get worse over time.

I've been working on my problems for years, but some of them just don't get better. Is it possible to learn to live with some of the symptoms of PTSD?

Yes. Many people have developed creative ways to manage their symptoms. For example, a person who suffers from insomnia might take on an extra job at night and make productive use of their time. A person who has developed a fear of open spaces after being attacked in the country might move to the city to reduce opportunities for anxiety. There are in fact all sorts of techniques available that can be used to manage some of the negative symptoms associated with PTSD. These include stress or anger management. Some of these techniques will be discussed elsewhere in the book.

Someone I know and care about has PTSD. What can I do to help?

As a concerned family member or friend, the most important thing you can do is to reassure the person of your love. You can also play an instrumental role in their recovery by helping them to secure therapy and by positively reinforcing the new and healthy behaviors that emerge. But a more difficult and absolutely essential step will be to stand aside, to allow them to take responsibility for themselves, their actions, and their recovery.

How do I find out more about PTSD?

Read through the rest of this book. In addition, there are dozens of other insightful books on PTSD which might help you better understand your condition. At the back of this book you will also find a list of suggested readings that may be useful. Attending a support group for people who have suffered similar trauma can also be a good form of self-education. Knowledge can be truly powerful over PTSD.

What steps can I take to facilitate my recovery from PTSD?

- Investigate and secure a therapist or support group that best suits your needs.
- Educate yourself as much as possible as to the nature of your condition.

- Work diligently with your therapist to design a treatment plan and attempt to follow it.
- Look after your physical health. Eat balanced meals, exercise regularly, get plenty of rest, and try out relaxation and other stress management techniques.
- Work hard to maintain intimate relationships and friendships and develop a network you can depend on.
- Avoid alcohol and illicit drugs.
- If you and your doctor agree to a trial of medication, take medications as prescribed. Many people do not do so. In addition, familiarize yourself with the common side effects and become attuned to the effects (both good and bad) that the medication actually has on you.
- It may be wise to avoid highly stimulating and violent movies and situations that can trigger off your symptoms.
- Understand that the recovery process may be slow, painful, and marked with disappointing setbacks. This is part of the deal for most people recovering from severe trauma. This does not mean that you and the therapy are failures.
- Be gentle with yourself.

References
Bufe, C. *Alcoholics Anonymous—Cult or Cure?*, Berkeley, Calif.: North Atlantic Books, 1996.

Chapter 7

TREATMENT OPTIONS FOLLOWING TRAUMA

How can I recover from trauma?

That depends on your situation. In this chapter we will outline treatment strategies that work for most people. It's important to keep in mind that there are many therapeutic approaches but only a few basic principles. Try to bear the principles in mind as you create your treatment strategy.

What's an example of a basic principle of treatment?

The basic principles we are talking about here are fundamental rules that apply to all therapies of PTSD. For example, all treatments need to foster a sense of trust and safety. Mistrust is a very common trait in people who have been traumatized and is often the reason why the therapeutic process can break down. It is important that you and your therapist be aware of this issue, because it impacts on other areas of treatment and on your recovery.

Are there other basic principles that I should be aware of?

Yes. In fact, Schwartz and Prout in 1991, noted five principles that could be part of any treatment for PTSD. They believe all treatments of PTSD should recognize that:

- after experiencing trauma, most victims tend to react to their situation in characteristic ways. Although these ways of reacting may be painful or perplexing, they are, under the circumstances, both common and normal.

- the relationship between the therapist and the victim should be collaborative, resulting in a greater sense of empowerment for the victim, whose dignity and security was diminished by the trauma.

- after a severe trauma, victims tend to avoid things that remind them of the trauma. Such avoidance can greatly diminish the person's quality of life. Treatment should therefore work to diminish this avoidance.

- victims of trauma need to rework their own story of the trauma.

- victims must be helped to integrate a sense of self lost or destroyed by the trauma.

How do I make use of these principles?

As an example, take a look at the first principle: People have characteristic responses to trauma. This may seem obvious, but if you are the one who has been severely traumatized, you may feel abnormal and alone. An important component of treatment is to try to educate you about trauma and help you recognize that your PTSD is not a bizarre reaction to stress. The educational issue is an important reason for this book, in fact, and is a key to all treatments, including prevention of PTSD in the first place.

Is there a way to prevent PTSD after a severe trauma?

Yes. Although it isn't possible to completely eliminate a stress reaction after severe trauma, it is possible that early intervention will prevent a full-blown PTSD from developing.

What kind of early support should I get?

Regardless of the type of trauma, victims are most frequently helped by friends and family, and it is essential to underscore the importance of familiar supports during times of stress. We are generally able to move beyond minor traumas without the need for help from "outsiders," and we should probably seek help first from those we know. When an entire community is destroyed, however, as might be the case after a flood or earthquake, everyone has been affected and few people may have the personal wherewithal to reach out and help others. Similarly, long-standing poverty or drug abuse can grind people down to the point that it becomes very difficult to reach out to the victim of an individual trauma. In addition, severe traumas often make the victim feel unreachable by his or her family and friends, regardless of how much they try to help. Not only do victims frequently feel alone after a trauma, but well-meaning family and friends may be left feeling impotent and unhelpful. Recovery takes patience and forbearance all the way around.

If you are a friend or family member of a trauma victim, know that it is extremely important that they have a clear understanding of what actually happened, and thus need to be given multiple opportunities to talk freely, in order to put their memories into perspective. Be aware, too, that memory often becomes impaired after a trauma, and it may be necessary to repeat basic information several times to someone who has either lost a loved one or been personally injured in some way.

If family and friends aren't enough, what else could be tried?

Just as family and friends can promote a feeling of safeness, so too can your surrounding culture or religion. Rituals, in particular, are very helpful. For example, Oscar's wife and daughter were killed in a traffic accident in which Oscar was the driver. Although he had not attended church in years, Oscar found great comfort in the gathering of friends and family at the wake and funeral, and solace in the familiar religious ritual. A generally unemotional man, Oscar was able to express his grief and guilt within these organized confines and was able to glean some hope that there was meaning in the premature deaths. To an outsider, rituals may seem meaningless. To the afflicted, rituals may be life saving.

However, it may be that none of the above techniques will prove useful for you and that securing professional help from a therapist will be necessary. Early psychological intervention can also help to prevent the development of full-blown PTSD following trauma.

We'll talk more about specific treatments later in the chapter, but it seems that there are a variety of ways to provide this sort of help. For example, one study showed that cognitive therapy, psychodynamic therapy, and hypnotherapy worked equally well in treating and preventing PTSD after one episode of trauma. For early interventions, groups are often quite useful.

I'm not a big fan of groups. Is group therapy necessary for people with post-traumatic stress disorder?

Seeing others in similar straits may help to convince you that you're not alone with your suffering and that you're not going crazy. It can also point you toward worthwhile recovery goals. If you are distrustful or frightened, however, a group may feel overwhelming.

As previously emphasized, safety and trust are paramount, and it may take a while before you feel comfortable exposing yourself to a group. If you do decide to try out group therapy, it is generally recommended that you join a group that is fairly homogeneous with regard to the type of trauma experienced. Don't worry if it seems that some people in your group have almost completely recovered from their trauma, while you still feel overwhelmed. People who are further along in recovery may be able to provide a sense of hope and guidance, giving you a feeling that you can get better.

Are there different kinds of group therapy?

Yes. Some groups tend to be educational, focusing on the course and symptoms of the disorder. This can be quite reassuring to both the victim and to family members because it can help to put the whole experience into perspective. This type of therapy tends to be fairly supportive and less anxiety provoking than other types of treatment.

Other groups focus on the patterns of thinking (cognition) and behaviors that have arisen as a result of the traumatic experience. Such groups might focus on a particularly troubling emotion, like anger, and work on ways to adapt to the troubling aspects of the emotion. Discussion of anger might lead to the exploration of related emotions, like rejection, fear, and distrust. This type of group tends to be fairly goal oriented and focused.

A process-oriented group might focus on the here and now of the people in the group, allowing sharing of experiences and gradual psychological exposure to traumatic memories. This type of group experience may be somewhat educational and may use some principles of cognitive-behavioral therapy, but the central experience has to do with emotional sharing, social support, and improved social functioning. However, in its effort to gain a corrective emotional experience, this type of treatment can be more anxiety provoking than the other group therapies.

So the leader of the group sets the tone for everybody else?

To some extent, that's true. However, the therapist and the group tend to create an interaction that works best for them. In addition, a crucial aspect of group therapy is that members learn from one another. The leader is important, but your participation counts even more.

What are support groups and how do they differ from group therapy?

Support groups differ from therapy groups in that there is no formal leadership. Instead, the group is run by the members themselves. Within this structured environment, members share their experiences, triumphs, and setbacks. They can also share up-to-date information about their condition and its treatment. It is a reciprocal process where members both give support to and receive support from the group. Being able to positively affect the lives of others is extremely powerful and serves to increase one's self-esteem. Support groups have become quite common in recent years, and you will probably be able to find one that specifically meets your needs. There are many groups for survivors of combat, incest, rape, and domestic abuse, for example, but there are also groups focused on just about every kind of trauma. Alcoholics Anonymous is a well-known support group.

Where can I find a support group that best suits my needs?

- Contact specific agencies or organizations that may deal with your particular situation, for example, agencies that deal with domestic violence or war veterans.
- Contact local hospitals or clinics for information.
- Use libraries or the Internet to search for contacts.
- Check newspapers and other periodicals (in the classified section).
- Check with the American Psychological Association or the American Psychiatric Association. Most major cities have local branches.
- The police department and victim assistance programs can also be helpful.

What's a survivor group?

Survivor groups are for people who have suffered trauma. These can be either support groups or therapy groups.

You've talked a lot about early interventions and groups. Where does individual therapy come in?

Seeing an individual therapist might be the first and only treatment that you need. We don't mention it first because some of the underlying principles can also be seen in crisis interventions and group therapies.

What are the different kinds of psychotherapy?

There are several different kinds of individual therapy, and, as with group therapies, they tend to overlap a good deal. In general, though, individual therapies can be divided into the following categories: supportive psychotherapy, cognitive-behavioral modification, and psychodynamic psychotherapy.

What is supportive psychotherapy?

Supportive psychotherapy is a form of talk therapy in which the therapist tends to support the person's characteristic ways of interacting with the world. Supportive therapists tend to be fairly interactive and tend to focus on the here and now rather than on issues from the past. They may provide a certain amount of guidance and may offer concrete advice when the need arises. The goal of therapy is to restore equilibrium rather than resolve unconscious conflicts. This type of therapy is commonly used for people with PTSD. After a severe trauma it may feel too raw and painful to explore feelings at great length, and support is vital. Virtually all treatments for PTSD should include supportive psychotherapy after the trauma and whenever symptoms become overwhelming. At the same time, further treatment is often necessary if recovery is going to be possible. Often, individual therapists begin treatment using supportive psychotherapy and then move on to other types of treatment as the situation evolves. At the same time, recovery from PTSD tends to ebb and flow, and when symptoms worsen, therapists tend to become, once again, more supportive.

What is cognitive-behavioral therapy?

"Cognitive-behavioral therapy" is an umbrella term that includes a variety of different treatments. What they have in common is the recognition that recovery doesn't necessarily require an investigation into the unconscious. Instead, there is a belief that internal change can follow behavioral or cognitive (thinking) change. These treatments use the concepts of supportive psychotherapy, especially with regard to the need for trust within the working relationship. They may also use psychodynamic concepts, especially regarding the maintenance of a healthy therapeutic relationship. Finally, they tend to be focused and time limited, which are often important considerations when you embark on a treatment.

What are examples of cognitive-behavioral treatments?

Cognitive-behavioral therapy can include treatments as varied as breathing exercises, biofeedback, systematic desensitization, flooding, and cognitive restructuring.

I've been breathing my whole life. You're suggesting that I need to take lessons?

We can all stand to improve our breathing. This is based on the fact that people who panic breathe shallowly, and that it is very difficult to be anxious if your breathing is strong and steady. A behavioral intervention might completely ignore the cause of your anxiety, but would instead focus on breathing techniques. For example, you might be asked to practice taking deep, steady breaths. This sounds simple but is a challenge for most of us. Try to watch your belly rise without moving your chest wall. Feel the air go in and out for a full minute. Practice this every day. If you can do it, you will probably find your anxiety decrease. The breath is vital, and there are whole schools of yoga that devote enormous energy to its study. Similarly, you might learn muscle relaxation techniques. Regardless of the cause of your muscle tension, you will feel more relaxed if your muscles are relaxed. Since anxiety is such a major problem, everyone with PTSD should practice steady breathing and muscle relaxation.

What is biofeedback?

Biofeedback is a form of relaxation education. While observing your own breathing, muscle tone, and general state of relaxation, you observe machines that are measuring these same physical/psychological states. The underlying theory is that people are better able to control their bodily responses if they are given immediate feedback. For example, as you get more anxious, your breathing becomes more rapid and shallow. The machine will begin to beep more rapidly, and you'll be reminded to deepen and slow your breathing, and your anxiety will lessen. People with PTSD have a strong tendency to lose control over these basic biologic processes, and you should consider any of these methods that help you regain a sense of control over your body.

What is systematic desensitization?

Systematic desensitization is a type of behavioral therapy that has been useful in the treatment of the avoidance behaviors that are so common in people with PTSD. After a specific problem is identified, the person with PTSD learns how to gradually approach the problem by becoming systematically desensitized to it. If you were, for example, in a terrible car wreck, and you are now afraid of driving, your therapist would help you approach the task of driving in a constructive, measured way. The therapist might ask you to rank several aspects of driving. For example, picking up your car keys might be fairly anxiety provoking, even if you are still in the house and have no intention of driving. You might practice picking up car keys while using relaxation exercises. You might then go out to the car with the car keys. The steps would proceed in a predictable manner: sitting in the car with the car keys, turning on the engine, driving down the driveway, etc. Each of these steps might take a session or more. For specific avoidance behaviors, systematic desensitization can be very helpful.

That seems pretty slow. Is there any behavioral technique that moves faster?

You might be interested in "flooding." Also known as implosive therapy, flooding is another behavioral technique used to desensitize persons to anxiety-producing stimuli. Instead of gradually being introduced to anxiety-producing stimuli, you would be bombarded by the images and memories that haunt you. For example, Sean is a war veteran who has been enduring terrible dreams and recollections of his combat experiences. He says he has no patience for all the talk therapies. He just wants to get rid of his symptoms. Sean's therapist agrees to try flooding him with frightening images in the hopes of desensitizing him to their power. They agree to set up a movie screening in which Sean watches the goriest segments of movies like *Saving Private Ryan, Full Metal Jacket,* and *Apocalypse Now.* In a successful treatment, Sean would be shaken up by the experience, but his intrusive memories would have lost their hold over him. As you might imagine, this technique is useful for only a small percentage of people with PTSD. The vast majority of people with PTSD find the idea of flooding to be assaultive and hurtful and have no interest in such a treatment.

You've mentioned behavioral therapies. What is cognitive therapy?

Also known as cognitive restructuring, cognitive therapy relies on the observation that how we think affects how we feel. The therapist helps the client examine some of the destructive thought patterns that have arisen as a result of the trauma. They would focus on the thought patterns that are unrealistic or inaccurate and that cause psychic pain. For example, after she was raped, Joyce kept thinking that she shouldn't have worn a sexy outfit that day, that she shouldn't have stopped to tell the rapist the time of day, and that she had somehow brought on the attack by having occasionally fantasized about being ravished by a mysterious stranger when she'd been a bit younger. These thoughts were making her feel guilty and miserable. The cognitive therapist might listen to these signs of Joyce's guilt and recognize that they are unreasonable. He might ally himself with Joyce's more rational side and point out that her thoughts are inaccurate. As the two of them work together, Joyce should see her thought patterns gradually evolve in a more healthy way and should then feel less burdened with guilt.

What I most need is for somebody to hear my whole story. How do I get that?

Any of the above therapists will probably be interested in hearing your story. Getting your feelings out can be very useful. As Shakespeare wrote in *Macbeth:* "Give sorrow words; the grief that does not speak whispers the o'erfraught heart and bids it break." Freud called the same thing "abreaction." We might call it "getting it off your chest."

I'm in a survivor support group and have talked about myself for the last six months. Several of the people in the group have been helped by cognitive-behavioral therapy, but when I tried it, I felt misunderstood. I need something more. Any suggestions?

You might try one of the psychodynamic psychotherapies. As with the cognitive-behavioral therapies, psychodynamic therapies include a variety of types of treatment. The hallmark of this type of treatment is that it focuses on the subjective experience of the victim of trauma. In other words, despite the similarity of symptoms, each victim of trauma is unique and will have his or her own characteristic style of dealing with the trauma. Psychodynamic therapy may address various aspects of the subjective experience, such as fantasies, fears, hopes, dreams, and guilt. It might help the victim elaborate his own sense of himself or his perceptions of others. An underlying belief of psychodynamic therapists is the existence of an unconscious, a part of ourselves that we may only be dimly aware of yet which tends to drive many of our feelings and behaviors.

How does psychodynamic psychotherapy help?

By sifting through feelings and memories, the client and therapist may begin to see patterns and themes that exist within the client. Recognition of an unhappy pattern is often the first step in changing that pattern. For example, Joe developed PTSD after having been severely beaten. When he came to therapy, he was not only suffering the typical symptoms of PTSD (avoidance, arousal, and reexperiencing) but was specifically terrified of getting into more fights. In his therapy, Joe recalled that he'd been in numerous fights during his life. He had always believed that the fights were thrust upon him, that he'd had no choice. As he talked about his fights, it became clear that he was unable to tolerate any signs of disrespect from other people and that he'd often thrown the first punch. His oversensitivity to disrespect seemed to stem from being picked on as a child. The therapy continued to focus on his current PTSD symptoms but also focused on the important issue of his oversensitivity and helped Joe recognize the fact that he could prevent fights by not being so sensitive to criticism and disrespect. In his therapy, Joe's rigid patterns were softened, and he could approach the world in a more flexible way.

I've heard about that kind of therapy. Doesn't it take years? And don't you have to go every day?

Psychoanalysis may require daily meetings for years, but traditional psychoanalysis would be an unusual recommendation for the typical person with PTSD. Instead, psychodynamic therapists make use of some of the principles of psychoanalysis in their efforts to help people, just as they use techniques from supportive and cognitive-behavioral therapies.

I agree that we're all unique and that talking is good. Who could possibly object to this kind of treatment?

Psychodynamic therapies tend to be more open-ended and less structured than other therapies. This can be a problem for people who have been traumatized. Talking about the experience can increase your level of anxiety, and you can end up feeling overwhelmed. There's a reason that your mind has split off the traumatic experience, and all therapies must pay careful attention to the issues of safety and protection during your recovery. A related issue is that it may be difficult for you to trust anyone, and psychodynamic therapies generally require a certain alliance with the therapist. To get better, however, it will be necessary to address your traumatic experiences in some way, and it will probably be necessary to talk to a therapist. For most people with PTSD, some sort of psychodynamic therapy will eventually be needed.

What kind of psychodynamic therapy works best for people with PTSD?

There is a good bit of controversy when it comes to specific psychotherapies for PTSD. You should probably seek out a well-trained therapist whom you feel comfortable with and who has experience with PTSD.

Good dynamic psychotherapists live all over the country, and fairly standard treatments can be successfully adapted to your particular issues. In addition, many types of group therapy are based on psychodynamic principles.

How long should dynamic psychotherapy take?

For most people with PTSD, dynamic therapies should be relatively brief and focused. This is particularly true if your trauma was a one-time event that occurred relatively recently. If your trauma occurred a long time ago, and you've had time to incorporate traumatic issues into your personality, therapy will probably take longer.

Are there any other new techniques that are being used to treat PTSD?

Yes, several. As we've said, PTSD has become increasingly recognized as a major health problem in this country and around the world, and many people have tried to come up with alternative treatments. In order to assess these treatments a symposium was held in 1993 that proposed that four treatments deserve a closer look: EMDR, VKD, TFT, and TIR. One of the requirements for the therapies observed and discussed at this symposium was that they had to be able to achieve results after a relatively short period of time (several weeks).

What's EMDR?

EMDR stands for Eye Movement Desensitization and Reprocessing. It is a form of treatment that was developed by Francine Shapiro in the late 1980s. EMDR makes use of principles from a variety of areas to specifically treat PTSD. EMDR might begin in much the same way as other therapies: gathering a history, discussing the traumatic event, and developing an alliance between the client and the therapist. The important difference is that the therapist will have the client move his or her eyes from right to left while thinking and talking about various aspects of the trauma. The eye movements seem to allow greater processing of the traumatic memories than is generally possible. As you may remember, one of the hallmarks of PTSD is that aspects of the trauma seem to get disconnected from the rest of the person's mind. The eye movements seem to bypass this disconnection and allow the thinking part of the mind to chew on these intense feelings.

How does EMDR work?

Nobody knows for sure how it works. Interestingly, there is a part of normal sleep in which we discharge lots of emotional energy through dreams. It is called rapid eye movement (REM) sleep. During REM sleep, our eyes naturally move back and forth. It may be that EMDR makes use of the same process that is used during dreaming.

It sounds so simple, so why doesn't everyone use it?

There is some controversy over its usefulness. Its proponents say that it is very effective and makes use of a unique technique (eye movements). They also point out that twenty thousand therapists have been trained to do EMDR and that it has been used all over the world. Because of its ability to get directly at traumatic pain, its proponents say that EMDR works quickly, often producing significant results in only a few sessions. Its detractors say that EMDR is standard psychotherapy that makes use of psychological exposure to trauma and that the eye movements don't contribute anything at all. They also point out that it is designed for people who have experienced a single trauma, whereas most people with PTSD have been traumatized more than once. No one seems to be saying that EMDR is ineffective. The concern is whether it is more effective than other treatments for acute post-traumatic stress. Studies are currently in progress that should help answer this important question.

What is VKD?

VKD stands for Visual Kinesthetic Dissociation. VKD is based on the observation that time seems to stand still for victims of trauma, leaving them stuck in traumatized mode, forcing them to relive and reexperience the trauma. Because they are stuck in that moment, they are unable to step out and look at the experience in an objective way. VKD helps teach the client to step outside of the event and view it as an outsider looking in. This sense of detachment allows a working through of the trauma without being overwhelmed.

How does VKD work?

VKD is clearly a type of psychodynamic therapy, and as such, treatment would proceed as it would with a more traditional therapy. The important distinction is that, at some point in the treatment, the therapist asks the client to "dissociate" and imagine they are watching a movie of their trauma being projected onto a screen. After watching the "movie" of the trauma, the client is instructed to imagine rewinding the movie and watching it over again at a faster speed. The therapist then asks what the client learned from the second viewing. The hope is that the client has developed a greater sense of empowerment after recognizing her ability to survive the trauma. The client might then be asked to pretend to communicate with her younger self and to reassure her that she will, indeed, survive the trauma.

VKD is thus a process that through dissociation and visualization enables the client to gain insight and empowerment.

What are the pros and cons of VKD?

Proponents of VKD say that it has been useful after only a single session. The client isn't forced to talk very much, since her main responsibility is to watch the intrapsychic movie, and this can be very helpful for people who get overwhelmed when they try to talk about their trauma. Detractors say that much of VKD is taken from more traditional therapies. In particular, they say that the development of detachment is the same as the development of an observing ego, a concept that has been around for many decades. The biggest clinical concern is that encouraging "dissociation" is risky with people who tend to get numb and detached under stress, and dissociation could make people worse. As with all therapies that are designed to be very brief, there may be inadequate time to develop an alliance with the therapist and so there may be inadequate trust when anxiety does become overwhelming.

What is TFT?

TFT stands for Thought Field Therapy. It is based on Chinese acupuncture. Proponents of TFT believe that the energy in our body flows along certain pathways called meridians. Illness is caused by blockages that lead to an imbalance of energy in certain parts of the body.

What happens during a TFT session?

The client thinks about the trauma or the associated symptoms while the TFT therapist applies pressure to vital points along the meridian.

Does TFT work?

Detractors dismiss the concept of energy meridians out of hand and point out that talking about trauma with an inexperienced therapist can do more harm than good. Proponents admit that there is no research to back up TFT, but they do point out that acupuncture has been proven to work for other ailments, and TFT relies on the same concept of energy meridians. They will also point to their satisfied clients. There has been minimal research on this sort of alternative treatment.

What is TIR?

TIR stands for Traumatic Incident Reduction. It is a form of systematic desensitization that focuses on the specific experience of the trauma victim.

What happens during TIR?

The treatment begins by the person with PTSD closing his eyes. The therapist then asks him to think about and visualize the incident. Unlike most treatments, the client with PTSD is asked not to say anything at first, just try to recall what happened. Once the client has done this, the therapist will start to ask for details of the event. The purpose of these questions is to encourage detailed recollections of the trauma. For example, the therapist might ask, "Where did the event take place?" or "What was the first thing you became aware of?" The traumatized person will try to visualize the events and report his experiences to the therapist, who listens to what is being said but makes no attempt to prompt the client or offer interpretations. Once this step has been completed, they repeat the process, with the therapist repeating these questions ten to twenty times.

How does TIR work?

As the traumatic event is mentally replayed, the person with PTSD recalls new details of the trauma and begins to interpret these details differently. The theory is that the trauma victim can gradually develop her own insight into the trauma and gradually decrease the intensity of the PTSD. As the traumatic event is reviewed, the mind can make more sense of it and gradually resolve the pain and conflict. In this way, it is a form of systematic desensitization.

What are the advantages and disadvantages of TIR?

Proponents of TIR say it encourages self-assertiveness and self-understanding, vital ingredients in the recovery from PTSD. Critics might point out that there are no studies to show that TIR works. In addition, critics might say that recalling the traumatic event could be quite painful without psychological support and without an experienced therapist helping to make sense of the devastating nature of the trauma. At this point, TIR is definitely in the "experimental" category.

I have found that drawing and writing about the trauma makes me feel better. Why is this?

Creative efforts can allow you to express the emotional impact of the trauma in a personal way. Pick what seems best for you. This may be a new activity that intrigues you or one that you've long loved. People are often helped by painting, drawing, writing, yoga, and dance, for example, but they are also helped by less obviously "creative" activities like carpentry, gardening, or basketball.

Is there such a thing as creative arts therapy?

Yes. For many decades, child psychoanalysts have used games and art in their efforts to draw out children. This practice has gradually spread to include the treatment of adults and is utilized in all sorts of settings. Within your individual therapy, you might be asked to keep a journal or write poems. Your therapist might want to look at your drawings. More commonly, however, your individual therapist won't ask about such things. Instead, you can practice these things on your own or you can look into getting a creative arts therapist. This is someone who is specially trained to work in this way. You might choose a therapist who specializes in such things as art, dance, drama, or music. These therapists have generally received a master's degree in their specialty and may be very useful in your recovery. The creative arts can remind you of what you most value in life.

I've heard about hypnosis. Is it useful?

Hypnosis has been used to treat victims of trauma for more than a century. Hypnosis induces an altered, relaxed state during which traumatic events can be recalled with less anxiety and stress. Some people block the trauma from conscious awareness, for example, and hypnosis can allow the therapist to uncover some previously unknown details. Hypnotic techniques can also be used, at times, for stress reduction, always an important issue for people with PTSD. There are drawbacks to hypnosis. While it may be useful for the therapist to know more about the trauma, the person with PTSD needs to be awake for the psychological exposure to work. In addition, people under hypnosis become more suggestible to the therapist's suggestions. This has led some vulnerable people to incorrectly remember the past, which is known as "false memory syndrome." False memory syndrome led to numerous false accusations of sexual abuse in recent years and led to most therapists becoming more careful when talking about sexual abuse that might or might not have happened a long time ago.

What medications are useful in PTSD?

While there is no single medication that works specifically for PTSD, there are a number of different types that are frequently prescribed and may help.

Frequently Prescribed Medication

- **Selective Serotonin Reuptake Inhibitors (SSRI's):** Medications in this category include Prozac, Zoloft, and Paxil. These are most commonly prescribed for major depression. In addition, they have been shown to reduce the numbing and hyperarousal symptoms among civilian trauma victims (van Der Kolk, Dryfuss, Michaels, et al., 1994). SSRI's may help reduce alcohol consumption, a frequent problem in people with PTSD (Brady, Sonne, and Roberts, 1995). Finally, these drugs may also help with rage, obsessional thinking, panic, and suicidality. There are other drugs related to the serotonin system, such as Buspirone, Trazadone, Nefazadone, and Cyproheptadine. Each of these medications has been shown to be effective with some people with PTSD. Serotonin drugs do have side effects, however, and the potential for insomnia can make this class less than perfect for people with PTSD

- **Monoamine Oxidase Inhibitors (MAOI's):** Examples include Nardil and Parnate. These drugs are most commonly used to treat depression. In PTSD, they seem to have helped best with reexperiencing symptoms, such as nightmares, flashbacks, and intrusive recollections. They don't seem to help other PTSD symptoms such as avoidance/numbing and hyperarousal (Southwick, Yehuda, Giller, et al., 1994). A particular drawback to Nardil and Parnate is the necessity for restrictions of diet and coprescribed medication. A new MAOI, Meclobemide, may renew interest in this class of medication, since it doesn't require the dietary and drug restrictions.

- **Tricyclic Antidepressants (TCA's):** Examples include Desipramine and Nortriptyline. These were the antidepressants of choice prior to the introduction of Prozac. While still used frequently, they are now generally used after other drugs have failed.

- **Antianxiety Drugs:** Known as benzodiazepines, examples include Valium, Klonopin, Ativan, Xanax, and Halcion. These drugs are frequently prescribed for anxiety, insomnia, and irritability. They tend to reduce anxiety but may not reduce core PTSD symptoms. While they are often helpful, you need to be aware of their risk of addiction and withdrawal symptoms. They can also worsen your feelings of being out of control.

- **Mood Stabilizers:** Originally used to treat seizures, examples include Tegretol and Valproate. There hasn't been much research with these medications in PTSD, but early results indicate that they are useful at reducing core symptoms such as hyperarousal, reexperiencing, and avoidance/numbing (Friedman and Southwick, 1995). While generally well tolerated, these medications require that you get blood drawn in order to check the levels of medication in your system and to ensure that your liver, kidneys, and blood are not being affected.

- **Antipsychotics:** Examples include Resperidone, Olanzepine, Haldol, Thorazine, and Mellaril. These drugs have been helpful with symptoms of PTSD such as agitation, fearfulness, and numbness.

- **Antiadrenergics:** Examples include Propranolol, Clonidine, and Guanfacine. While not used as frequently as some of the drugs already listed, there is evidence that this class of medication may be the most helpful in treating PTSD. (Friedman, 1998). The adrenergic part of the nervous system is responsible for arousal, anxiety, reexperiencing, and some aspects of rage and dissociation. These medications can be directly helpful in stabilizing the intensity of these feelings, all of which are central to PTSD.

How long do medications take to work?

It varies. All of the antidepressants take at least a few weeks, as do the mood stabilizers. The antianxiety and antipsychotic drugs may work immediately. Antiadrenergic medications fall somewhere in between.

Will I need to take medication forever?

Probably not, though this is something you will need to talk over with your doctor. In general, antidepressant medications need to be taken at least six months after your depression has lifted, and many psychiatrists suggest a year. Other medications are more variable.

Is it true that some medications affect sexual performance?

Yes. Some psychiatric medications can diminish the ability to become sexually aroused, maintain the arousal, and/or have an orgasm. There are often ways to deal with this problem. If you are having any sexual problems, whether or not you think they're related to your medication, you should talk them over with your psychiatrist.

If I take medication, will I need to stay away from alcohol, marijuana, and any other stimulants?

Yes, this is advisable. Alcohol and other stimulants such as marijuana can react negatively with certain medications and can also worsen your symptoms of depression, detachment, and anxiety.

There seem to be a lot of treatments for PTSD. I still don't have a good handle on how they actually work. Any suggestions?

In the next chapter, we explore ways in which people have actually been helped. Read on.

References

Allen, S. N., and S. L. Bloom. "Group and Family Treatment of Post-Traumatic Stress Disorder" in *Psychiatric Clinics of North America,* 17:2, June 1994, pp. 425–437.

Brady, K. T., S. C. Sonne, and J. M. Roberts. "Sertraline Treatment of Comorbid Post-Traumatic Stress Disorder and

Alcohol Dependence." *Journal of Clinical Psychiatry* 56, 1995, pp. 502–505.

Brom, D., R. J. Kleber, and P. B. Defares. "Brief Psychotherapy for Post-Traumatic Stress Disorders." *Journal of Consultation and Clinical Psychology* 1989, pp. 607–612.

Chertoff, J. "Psychodynamic Assessment and Treatment of Traumatized Patients." *Journal of Psychotherapy Practice and Research* 7:1, Winter 1998, pp. 35–46.

Friedman, M. J. "Current and Future Drug Treatment for Post-Traumatic Stress Disorder Patients." *Psychiatric Annals* 28:8, 1998, pp. 461–468.

Friedman, M. J., and S. M. Southwick. "Towards Pharmacotherapy for PTSD." In M. J. Friedman, D. S. Charney, and A. Y. Deutch, eds., *Neurobiological Clinical Consequences of Stress: From Normal Adaptation to PTSD.* Philadelphia: Lippincott-Raven, 1995, pp. 465–481.

Rose, D. S. "Worse Than death: Psychodynamics of Rape Victims and the Need for Psychotherapy." *American Journal of Psychiatry* 143, 1986, pp. 817–824.

Schwartz, R. A., and M. F. Prout. "Integrative Approaches in the Treatment of Post-Traumatic Stress Disorder." *Psychotherapy* 28, 1991, pp. 364–373.

Southwick, S. M., R. Yehuda, E. L. Giller, et al. "Use of Tricyclics and Monoamine Oxidase Inhibitors in the Treatment of PTSD: A Quantitative Review." In: M. M. Marburg, ed., *Catecholamine Function in Post-Traumatic Stress Disorder: Emerging Concepts.* Washington, DC: American Psychiatry Press, 1994, pp. 293–305.

van Der Kolk, B. A., D. Dryfuss, M. Michaels, et al. "Fluoxetine in Post-Traumatic Stress Disorder." *Journal of Clinical Psychiatry* 55, 1994, pp. 517–522.

Chapter 8

HOW THERAPY IS APPLIED—FIVE STORIES

In the first chapter, we introduced you to four people who suffer from PTSD: Jim, Lilly, Fred, and Beverly. In this chapter, we are going to discuss their lives in more detail. These four people were chosen because their treatments reflect many of the important issues in PTSD. If you or a loved one has symptoms of PTSD, it is unlikely that any one of these people will exactly match your situation. Nevertheless, these four have experienced much of the pain and possibility that tend to exist in people with PTSD.

How do you plan to make use of those examples from the first chapter?

Let's start with Jim, the Vietnam veteran, whom we met on page 8. As you may remember, he was upset about his nightmares and insomnia, but he was especially concerned that his wife might leave him. At the time of this crisis, he was forty-nine years old and had been married to Eve for twenty years. They had two teenage children. He was willing to do anything to save his marriage, and his wife convinced him to go to couple's counseling. This was an important event for Jim. He had suffered from his PTSD for thirty years and was only now coming for treatment. He did not see himself as having PTSD, however. He saw himself as having a sleep problem that had worsened after his internist had refused to give him any more sleeping medication. His wife felt that his main problem was the fact that he drank two six-packs of beer every night and that he was always tired and irritable. They described these problems to the therapist, who said that no psychological work could be done until Jim quit drinking alcohol.

So the therapist wasn't even going to treat his PTSD?

The therapist decided that Jim's alcoholism would interfere with any treatment for PTSD, and so the therapist recommended a consultation at an alcohol rehabilitation center. As you can imagine, Jim was none too pleased with this suggestion. He believed that his wife had set him up, which enraged him. Nevertheless, he believed that his wife might leave him this time, so he agreed to the consultation. The psychiatrist at the alcohol rehabilitation center agreed with the therapist, especially after he heard that Jim had tried to stop drinking a number of times in the past without success. This psychiatrist suggested that Jim go into the hospital for detoxification and rehabilitation. Jim knew that he drank too much, but he still felt that his insomnia justified whatever alcohol he drank, and he felt deeply misunderstood and angry. At this point many people would have gone home and tried to continue their lives. Under the threat of a divorce, however, Jim agreed to the hospitalization. He was pleasantly surprised that his employer gave him paid leave and that his insurance company would cover almost the entire bill.

How did the hospitalization go for Jim?

The hospitalization was difficult. In order to prevent severe alcohol withdrawal, Jim was given Librium, a drug that is in the same family as Valium, and so the withdrawal wasn't as bad as it had been when he'd tried to stop on his own. He wasn't too keen on the group therapy sessions in the beginning. Not only was he preoccupied by being in a hospital and by his alcohol withdrawal, he didn't feel that he had very much in common with most of the other people in the unit. They all seemed young and tended to do a lot of drugs in addition to drinking alcohol. Once a week, though, there was an AA meeting that was attended mostly by veterans, and that became the highlight of his week. Even after he left the rehab, he drove forty-five minutes every Wednesday night to get to that AA meeting. Jim found that these guys understood something of what he was going through. Their stories matched up with his in a lot of ways.

After a few weeks in the hospital, his mind began to clear up, and he found that he could read and concentrate better than he could remember. His nightmares and insomnia were still there, and he felt more wound up and irritable than he'd been at home. He would've checked out of the hospital in a minute, except that his wife held to the threat of divorce. As part of the hospitalization, his therapist began to have sessions with him and his wife and other sessions with the whole family. These felt like torture. While they told him they loved him and that they were proud of his recent efforts, they also told him the extent to which they were scared of his moods. His daughter revealed that she'd never felt comfortable bringing friends home because she never knew when he'd blow up. His son wouldn't say much in the sessions and wouldn't even look him in the eye. They all told him that he was distant and difficult. He wished he'd never come into the hospital.

Did things get better for Jim?

After a month in the hospital his detoxification was complete, and he began to get specific treatment for his PTSD. First, he was told his diagnosis. He'd heard of PTSD, of course, and he knew that a couple of his Vietnam buddies had gotten it. He'd just never believed the diagnosis fit him. Now that he was getting some specific information, it was clear that he had PTSD. Knowing the diagnosis allowed him to put some of his symptoms into perspective. He wasn't just grouchy and explosive, he had the overarousal and anxiety of PTSD. He didn't just have nightmares, he was reexperiencing his Vietnam traumas. It wasn't just that he was distant and difficult, he was avoiding intimacy. This last symptom didn't make much sense at first, since he loved his family more than anything. Jim gradually understood that he'd distanced himself from his family at least partly because he was afraid of losing the people around him and that this was related to watching his two best friends get killed in the war. Alcohol served to relax him and help him sleep, but it also worsened his moods and increased the distance between him and his family. While much work remained to be done, Jim felt some relief that he was making progress.

What else was going on besides individual therapy?

While therapy was being begun, a psychiatrist had evaluated him and prescribed clonidine, which is a drug that specifically reduces symptoms of overarousal. Clonidine is often a good choice for people like Jim, since it can specifically treat PTSD symptoms without the risk of addiction. The clonidine turned out to be quite effective at reducing Jim's overarousal, and within ten days he began to notice a gradual decrease in his edginess.

They'd tried to teach Jim ways to more effectively breathe and relax when he'd first entered the hospital, but he hadn't paid much attention. As he began to talk about his PTSD, he found that these relaxation techniques were helpful and important.

What worked best for Jim?

All of his treatments played an important role. It was vital that Jim get an intensive treatment for his alcoholism, a treatment that he wouldn't have gotten without pressure from his wife. It was important that his family have a chance to talk over their feelings with him. The clonidine was useful. He needed to know that he had a PTSD diagnosis, and he needed to know what that diagnosis meant. He was then ready to treat his PTSD.

You mean he hasn't started his treatment yet?

There are a series of treatments that may be required for a complicated problem like Jim's. He'd made important strides toward recovery, but he wasn't there yet. For most people, recovery from PTSD requires some form of reexposure to the traumatic memories and a working through of the feelings surrounding these memories. That began in the week prior to his discharge from the hospital. While he continued to talk to his individual therapist, he found that group therapy worked best for him. As we mentioned, he'd enjoyed his AA group, and by his third week in the hospital he began to attend a support group that was specifically focused on Vietnam veterans who had PTSD. It was helpful for Jim to see other veterans who'd almost completely recovered from PTSD. It was also helpful for him to help out some guys who were considerably worse off than he was. It was painful to hear the stories of the other men, and even more painful to tell his own stories, but he'd finally found a place where his experiences wouldn't be considered bizarre and horrible. It was in this way that he could practice reexposure and working through.

What ended up happening with Jim?

He continued all of the treatments we outlined above. He continued to be fairly moody, but he wasn't as explosive. His nightmares diminished after a few months, though he still had a bad dream every week or two. He remained fairly tense, but he became much more adept at noticing the things that triggered his edginess in the first place. Noticing the triggers let him manage them more effectively. From his perspective, he was most pleased the following January. His wife had given him a woodworking set for Christmas. He'd enjoyed carpentry when he'd been a teenager, but he'd not had the time or inclination to pursue any hobbies since starting a family. In fact, he realized he'd enjoyed very little since coming back from Vietnam. As he was fooling around with a piece of wood one day, his son came out and asked if he'd show him how to use the tools. As they sat down to carve a piece of wood, Jim realized that life was, in a way, more painful than it had been. Without the alcohol to numb him, he felt more of the small stresses of life, and he'd learned that his PTSD might not ever completely disappear. At the same time, his treatment had allowed him the chance to get acquainted with his son in a way that had not previously been possible. Jim knew it was a fair trade-off.

Jim's case may represent a lot of issues that relate to PTSD, but my situation seems very different from his. My trauma happened fairly recently, for one thing, and I don't have an alcohol problem. Do you have an example that might fit my situation?

Let's take a look at Lilly. In the first chapter, we learned that she had developed PTSD after having been raped. For six months following the attack, she avoided reminders of the attack as best she could, but she still found herself frequently shaking with fear. She'd become increasingly isolated and felt unable to let anyone touch her, much less get more physically intimate. After six months of this, she recognized that she needed to seek treatment, but she didn't know where to turn. She'd graduated from college a few months before the rape and was working in a science lab as a way to assess whether or not she wanted to go to medical school. She was living in a city that was five hundred miles from home, and she had no close friends there. This worsened her sense of isolation, as had her decision not to worry her family about the fact that she'd been raped. She figured she needed to see a therapist, but she felt too scared to talk to anyone.

How did Lilly ever get into treatment?

It was a gradual thing. Lilly became friendly with another woman in her lab, who invited her to come to a yoga class that was being held nearby. The yoga consisted of some fairly intense stretching, and Lilly realized that she'd had hardly any exercise since leaving college. It felt pretty good to get back in touch with her body. In addition, much of the class centered on breathing practice, and that seemed to calm her. At the end of the class there was a five-minute meditation session, and Lilly was surprised to find that she could hold still for only a few seconds before horrible memories of the rape forced her to leave the room. Despite the anxiety she sometimes felt in the yoga class, Lilly began to attend the class several times a week. She was gradually able to tell her friend that something terrible had happened to her, and the friend steered her to a therapist who was sympathetic to meditation and breathing exercises.

What kind of therapy did they do?

They did a combination of supportive psychotherapy, behavior modification, and psychodynamic psychotherapy. The first few sessions were spent discussing various topics related to Lilly's life. Whenever she tried to talk about the rape, Lilly found herself choking up, getting scared and changing the subject. The therapist worked with her on breathing exercises and muscle relaxation techniques, and they gradually formed more of an alliance. Lilly wasn't sure if the therapy was doing anything, but she was able to hold still in meditation sessions for longer periods of time and was better able to keep her breathing steady.

When did they get round to talking about the rape?

It wasn't until the fifth session that Lilly was able to tell the whole story of the rape. While doing so, she mainly felt numb. The therapist asked her to repeat the story, and she was able to recall a few more details that she had previously forgotten. She left the session feeling frozen. Upon returning home, she collapsed on her bed, feeling tired, scared, and humiliated. After canceling the next two sessions, Lilly was able to restart treatment. While apologetic for not coming to the sessions, Lilly had known that she needed a break. Such ups and downs continued over the next several months, and she sometimes wondered if she should quit therapy. Nevertheless, she knew that she was getting better at talking about her feelings and memories about the rape.

What did they talk about during her sessions?

They talked about what had happened and how it had affected her life and her hopes for the future. They talked about how it had felt at the time and how she'd developed a fear of men. Sometimes she'd describe how angry she was that he'd never been caught. At other times she talked about how disgusting she felt. She talked about her fear that she'd been infected with the AIDS virus. With her therapist's support she got herself tested and was relieved to find out that she had contracted no diseases. She also became aware that she feared her genitals had been damaged during the attack. She knew enough to realize that this was unlikely, but she decided to go ahead and see a gynecologist, who reassured her. She became intrigued by the science of PTSD. In particular, she became curious about how talking about her feelings and memories could lead to psychological and biological changes in her, and this helped her feel more optimistic. She'd actually forgotten that she had once been an optimistic person, and glimmerings of optimism were a big relief.

How did her life change outside of therapy?

She continued to go to yoga classes and became much more aware of how tight her body had become. She practiced meditation and breathing exercises in order to get better at being relaxed and calm. She noticed that she'd been spending all of her free time alone, and she made efforts to change this pattern. She went on a couple of yoga retreats and signed up for a pottery class at the local college and even went on a date. She considered moving back to her hometown to be nearer to her old friends and family, but these new activities had set her up with new friends. In addition, her sister decided to move to the same city, which would allow them to be roommates. When Lilly did tell her sister about the sexual assault, she felt like she was going to fall apart. But she didn't, and they developed a new-found closeness.

How did things end up going for Lilly?

After six months of therapy, Lilly no longer had PTSD. While she still had a few symptoms, they didn't intrude on her life. She decided to continue her psychotherapy to work on some other issues and was essentially able to put the rape behind her.

My situation is more like Fred's, the paramedic. How was he treated?

When we left Fred, he was struggling to deal with the aftereffects of witnessing a tragic bus disaster. After two months he remained unable to rid himself of his horrible memories. He could occasionally calm himself, but there were so many triggers for his anxiety that he was almost always cycling between feeling numb and being frightened. He moved to Florida, where he hoped there might be fewer reminders of the accident. While Florida lacked cliffs and snow, he would never be able to avoid all buses and children. And then he and his wife discovered she was pregnant. They'd been trying to get pregnant for two years, and Fred would ordinarily have been overjoyed. Two months into his PTSD, however, all he could think of was the possibility that his own child could be in an accident.

What did they do?

Fred's desperation led his wife to seek out treatment for him, and they went together for his first appointment to a psychologist. The first session was designed to let Fred tell his story, and the therapist discovered that Fred had always been outgoing and confident, and that this disaster had completely unraveled him. He discovered that Fred had never abused drugs or alcohol, had never been depressed or especially anxious, and had been looking forward to having kids all his life. Within the first session, the psychologist told them that Fred's situation was ideal for behavior modification, and that they would begin during the next session.

How did therapy go for Fred?

First, the therapist practiced a few relaxation techniques with him. Fred had no trouble with these. In fact, he felt fine when he was in the therapist's office, as long as he didn't talk about the accident. This is an important issue in the treatment and contrasts somewhat with the other three cases. While his PTSD had disturbed Fred's equilibrium, his sense of trust in the world was essentially intact. Even when he began talking about the accident, he never mistrusted the therapist. He became anxious and cried at numerous points in the telling of his story, but he was able to make a rapid, comfortable bond with the therapist.

What difference does it make that Fred was easily able to trust the therapist?

As we've pointed out, most experts agree that treatment for PTSD requires a psychological reexposure to the traumatic memories. To tolerate such an activity, it is generally necessary to trust the therapist. In addition, it is necessary to trust that you possess the ability to deal with the crippling feelings that such exploration evokes. In our first example, Jim's treatment was complicated by his alcoholism and by the long-standing nature of his PTSD. Both of these issues complicate treatment because they stymie interpersonal skills and interpersonal trust. Our second case, Lilly, was slow to recover because the rape was intensely wounding to her sense of self. Being alone in a new city, she responded to the assault by closing herself off. These responses also complicate treatment. And for the woman whom we will meet next, Beverly, childhood abuse had affected much of her sense of self and had led to a strong baseline level of mistrust. And that complicates treatment. Fred had none of these issues.

So what happened with Fred's therapy?

Fred was able to begin talking about the accident during the second session, and although his story was very sad and horrifying, he didn't feel as overwhelmed as he'd thought he would. After a few sessions of this, he began to feel a need to talk about his wife's pregnancy and his fears for his unborn child. Continued talk therapy was very helpful, and Fred's symptoms almost completely lifted within six weeks.

The last person you described in the first chapter was Beverly. You said her situation was complicated. How did her treatment go?

As described on page 10, Beverly had begun a treatment for depression and ended up with overpowering memories of having been sexually molested as a child. Hers is the kind of situation that tends to confuse a lot of people.

How does Beverly qualify for PTSD?

Even though she'd blocked out its memories, Beverly had clearly been traumatized by the abuse. In addition, she described each of the three cardinal symptoms of PTSD, and it seemed likely that her current problems were directly related to that trauma. Her constant tension was a sign of overarousal. The creepy feelings of hands all over her was an example of reexperiencing the trauma. Finally, she not only avoided physical intimacy because it caused that uncomfortable physical feeling, but she'd spent most of her life avoiding even the memory of her molestation. She had all the cardinal symptoms: overarousal, reexperiencing, and avoidance.

How can someone forget being sexually abused as a child?

It may seem impossible, but it's a fairly common occurrence. It sometimes happens because the child was victimized before she'd developed good language skills, and so the memory is imprinted by way of feelings rather than words. It can also happen to anyone who is overwhelmed. If so, it would be more accurate to say that the person was blocking the memory rather than simply forgetting it. We forget things all the time, but they are mostly trivial memories. If we forget something important—like abuse—our minds have decided to actively block the memory from our awareness. The memory finds other ways to come out, as in Beverly's creepy feeling, and the memory never really goes away.

How do you treat somebody like Beverly?

The basic principles apply to all people with PTSD. It's important for all people with PTSD (including Beverly) to develop a sense of trust in both the therapist and in the therapeutic process. It's important to develop ways to soothe yourself and relax. And it is necessary to safely reexpose yourself to the traumatic memories and their corresponding feelings so that their impact can become more moderate and reasonable. Each of these issues was difficult for Beverly.

Why would Beverly have an especially hard time?

It's hard to develop basic trust in a therapist if your trust has been violated as a child. Not only did Beverly's stepfather molest her, but her mother was unable to protect her. From Beverly's point of view, it wasn't all that important whether or not her mother even knew about the abuse: to a child, it generally feels that the mother must know and must have given her approval. It is typical for abused children to feel that there is no option but to accept the abuse. The helplessness and hopelessness they feel about their situation feeds into the numbness and sense of unreality of PTSD. Like many adults who were molested as children, Beverly developed a powerful sense that other people couldn't be trusted. We can see this in her distrust of her therapist, but we can also see it in her inability to maintain romantic relationships.

If trust is so important, is there any hope for Beverly?

The child's sense of trust can be damaged but can't be completely crushed. As her therapy continued, Beverly became increasingly able to believe in the good intentions of her therapist. She was especially affected by the fact that her therapist seemed able to tolerate whatever ugliness or rage she brought to the session. She'd always assumed that if she were honest about her feelings, the other person would either hurt her or vanish. Her levels of trust and safety definitely fluctuated, but their relationship felt increasingly real and powerful.

What else did they do besides develop a relationship?

They talked about the molestation, for one thing. Beverly felt relieved to expose her memories and feelings to the light of day, but these talks were also anxiety provoking and painful. It was difficult to get beyond the feeling that talking about the molestation was traumatic and pointless, but she persevered. The two of them also talked about how the abuse had led to her current symptoms. Beverly found it especially helpful to know that her symptoms weren't crazy but were derived from reasonable responses to unreasonable situations. As she learned to recognize her symptoms of overarousal, avoidance, and reexperiencing, she began to see that she'd arranged her whole life to deal with these symptoms of PTSD. Recognizing her patterns led to some changes in her behavior and to a greater sense of control and mastery.

How did she see changes in her life?

She felt calmer and less depressed. Some of this might have been due to her antidepressant medication, but she also felt she was seeing the world in a different way. When she got stressed out, she was less prone to panic and outrage and was better able to think through the problem. She developed a relationship and got engaged. The world felt like a more open place. She was still bothered by the creepy feeling at times, but it didn't bother her very often and she didn't let it control her life.

So she lived happily ever after?

Beverly lives in the real world, and nobody around here lives happily ever after. There are always going to be stumbling blocks. In Beverly's case, her wedding turned out to be a crisis. After having worked through many of her issues with her therapist and getting engaged, she ended the treatment. Planning for the wedding involved significant interaction with her mother, a person she'd not spent much time with since moving away from home. Their frequent interaction led to a relapse into some of the PTSD symptoms. She was quite upset about this, having hoped that her PTSD was behind her. Beverly restarted therapy, and her therapist pointed out that weddings are classic times for mother-daughter issues to get played out, and that one reoccurrence did not put her back at square one. Beverly was back to her healthier self by the time of the wedding. Since getting married, Beverly hasn't had serious PTSD symptoms.

You've talked a lot about the treatment for individuals after a trauma. What about treating whole populations after a natural disaster?

The principles are the same. Let's look at a typical disaster and try to notice all the different interventions. There was a terrible earthquake in Armenia in 1988. Four cities and 350 towns were destroyed, and at least twenty-five thousand people were killed. Some doctors from UCLA created an outreach program to help some of the people in that country. They worked with students in the second-largest city in Armenia, Gumri, a city in which 7 percent of the population was killed and half the buildings were destroyed. The members of this particular outreach team performed a variety of tasks that have become fairly standard, and they talked to all students, not just those who seemed most affected. They intervened only after the city had dug itself out from the rubble and the teenagers had re-created something of their old lifestyles. All the students received four half-hour group sessions and an average of two one-hour individual sessions, which were conducted over a three-week period. In the group setting, the American psychiatrists asked the students to talk about their earthquake experiences and current problems. Then they had the children draw pictures of their earthquake experiences, their families, the city before the earthquake, and how they perceived the city of the future. The visiting psychiatrists used the pictures to explore various issues that are related to PTSD: avoidance, distortions, omissions, misattributions, and other aspects of memory and emotion. In the group setting, students were encouraged to talk about their loss and grief, which allowed group members to recognize the common elements of bereavement, such as disbelief, reunion fantasies, and preoccupations with the memories of last interactions with people who had died. Efforts were made to restore a more balanced and healthy view of their deceased family and friends. As the classroom sessions continued, the children talked about how the disaster had interfered with their lives and aspirations, and they talked about the practical realities of managing aggression and dealing with school and family. They were taught relaxation techniques (e.g., controlled breathing and muscle relaxation). In individual sessions, the children talked about their most significant traumatic moments and how those moments were linked with current distress. In particular, they were helped to notice traumatic reminders that surrounded them. These traumatic reminders were common causes of the core symptoms of PTSD: avoidance, arousal, and reexperiencing the event. Toward the end of their intervention, the psychiatrists helped the children take another look at their most traumatic memories and reframe them in terms of helplessness and conflict. Finally, as they prepared to return to the United States, the therapists explored termination issues with the children, because endings are often a time for the reemergence of issues, especially in people who have been traumatized by loss and death.

Did their efforts do any good?

When they compared the group that had been helped with a group that had received no intervention, the doctors found that their interventions were very effective at reducing post-traumatic stress. Three additional points about this study warrant mention: The first is that the therapy team didn't start their intervention until eighteen months after the disaster. The city had needed that much time to rebuild itself into some semblance of normalcy, and the initial mental health efforts had been directed at the most seriously afflicted. Nevertheless, despite the delay, their efforts were very helpful. The second point is that many people were helped despite a fairly small amount of face-to-face contact. The final major point is that we don't know which of the interventions was most helpful. The doctors tried everything they could think of, and some interventions, or combination of interventions, helped most of the children. As you try to figure out what might help you—or your loved one—remember that there is a lot of overlap between different therapies, even if we tend to separate them into different categories. In other words, effective psychodynamic therapy and effective cognitive-behavioral therapy are often more similar than they are different.

They waited eighteen months before they treated the children in Armenia. Isn't it better to intervene right away?

Much of the decision depends on psychological readiness. While it is never too early to provide for safety and comfort, victims of trauma may take a while to be ready to make use of talking therapies.

My situation doesn't have anything to do with an earthquake in Armenia. Can any of the principles be applied to my case?

Absolutely. We chose the intervention in Armenia to underscore the point that there is a cluster of emotional reactions that tends to occur immediately after traumas, whether the trauma occurred in Oklahoma City or on the other side of the world. If you are suffering from the symptoms of PTSD, remember that you aren't alone out there. Many people have been traumatized, and, just as importantly, many people have recovered.

References

Chemtob, C. M., S. Tomas, W. Law, et al. "Postdisaster Psychosocial Intervention: A Field Study of the Impact of Debriefing on Psychological Distress." *American Journal of Psychiatry* 154:3, March 1997, pp. 415–417.

Goenjian A. K., I. Karayan, R. S. Pynoos, et al. "Outcome of Psychotherapy Among Early Adolescents after Trauma," *American Journal of Psychiatry* 154:4, April 1997, pp. 536–542.

Chapter 9

FACTS ABOUT
SPECIFIC TRAUMAS

This chapter will address some of the commonly asked questions regarding specific traumas, including rape and sexual abuse, domestic violence, war and combat, and natural disasters. The chapter will also cover issues pertaining to children suffering from PTSD, with a focus on child abuse and incest.

RAPE AND SEXUAL ABUSE

What is rape?

Rape is forced sexual intercourse without consent. Legal definitions of rape conclude that some form of penetration must occur.

What constitutes sexual abuse?

The definition of sexual abuse is much broader than that of rape. Sexual abuse includes any form of unwanted sexual activity, such as touching, petting, forced masturbation, forced voyeurism, and forced undressing. Forced oral, anal, and vaginal intercourse, although classified as rape, would also fall under the broader umbrella of sexual abuse.

Why do people commit sexual abuse?

This is a difficult question to answer, because there are no hard-and-fast rules. Sexual abuse is, however, an act of power, where one person seeks to dominate another. In some instances the end result is to achieve sexual gratification, but this is not typical. In most cases, abusers are attempting to inflict harm on others, to induce feelings of degradation or humiliation, to subjugate others, or to instill in themselves a false sense of strength or power.

Is it possible to tell if a person has the potential to be sexually abusive?

While there are no certainties, sexual abusers tend to have the following characteristics:

- display physically aggressive or violent behaviors toward you or toward others.
- have poor frustration tolerance, becoming easily incited to bouts of inappropriate anger.
- have a negative attitude toward women.
- try to coerce you into engaging in activities that you don't want to do, such as drinking, taking drugs, or engaging in unprotected sex.
- display extremely dominating behaviors in other areas of life.
- tend to bully or verbally abuse others who are younger or weaker than they are, including children, seniors, and even animals.
- have an abnormal fascination with weapons.

How common is sexual abuse?

As a victim of sexual abuse, you may feel alienated and alone, but in reality, recent statistics show that sexual abuse is common. Some studies estimate that as many as one in four women (odds are a little lower for men) will experience some form of sexual abuse in their lifetime. Exact statistics are difficult to determine because of the sensitive nature of the assault. Even though contemporary men and women are more likely to come forward and report incidents of sexual abuse, powerful myths that surround rape and sexual abuse continue to impede the reporting of such crimes.

Are young attractive women more likely to be raped than older or unattractive women?

No. Statistics show that age or physical appearance have no bearing on whether a person is raped. Unattractive, overweight, and elderly women are raped just as frequently as others. Rape is generally a random act committed as an act of domination and not out of sexual desire. In this society great emphasis is placed on maintaining our physical beauty, and yet women who dress seductively or provocatively are more likely to be blamed for inviting the assault than those who dress with modesty. But don't be fooled into accepting this myth as fact. Dressing in a certain fashion in no way suggests that you are asking to be raped. You have the right to say no to any form of sexual activity at any time. And even if you willingly had intercourse with someone on a previous occasion, they do not have the right to coerce you into having sexual intercourse with them again.

Is it true that you can't be raped by someone you know?

No. Rape is rape regardless of whether the person is a stranger, an acquaintance, your friend, your neighbor, your date, your lover, or even your spouse. In fact, because of the violation of trust, being raped by someone you know can be even more damaging than being raped by a complete stranger. Date rape, a phenome-

non that is getting a fair amount of news coverage
these days, is very common, particularly on college
campuses.

How often does male rape occur?

This is difficult to determine because there is very little
documented information regarding the types and incidents of male rape. It seems that men are even less
likely to report rapes than women. This reluctance
could be related to fear of public humiliation and also
to the fact that much male rape occurs in institutions,
such as prison.

Is it true that men can only be raped by other men and not by women?

While uncommon, women can rape men, often
through a combination of intimidation and coercion.
Despite the psychological discomfort, physical stimulation during a rape will often lead to genital arousal in
both men and women.

Does experiencing a sexual response during the rape or other forms of sexual abuse mean that I enjoyed it and really wanted it to happen?

Absolutely not. The genital area is comprised of sensitive muscle tissues that are capable of involuntarily responding to sexual stimulation. In some instances,
abusers go out of their way to stimulate a sexual response in their victims, even bringing them to orgasm.
An involuntary bodily response to an act of violence
should not be confused with desire.

Sometimes I fantasize that a handsome stranger carries me off on a white horse and forces himself on me in a

beautiful meadow. Does this mean I secretly want to be raped?

No, dreams are not reality. People use fantasy and day-dreaming as a way of releasing tension or helping themselves to feel good, but they are seldom associated with real life. Rape and other forms of sexual abuse imply that the victim has no control over the situation. When you fantasize and when you daydream, you are essentially still in control. The above fantasy suggests a dreamy, romantic feeling and a desire to be passive during a sexual encounter that you intend to enjoy. This is quite different from wanting to be raped.

During an attack, is it better to fight back or to remain passive?

There is no set way of reacting to a violent attack. How one responds to a situation is based on the particular set of circumstances at the time, including whether the attacker has a weapon. It is also related to how the body's defense mechanism responds *(fight, flight, or freeze)*.

Some people feel guilty about not fighting back, while others who may have been seriously injured during an attack feel that perhaps they should have remained passive. The truth is, your reaction while the attack was occurring is really irrelevant to the fact that you were severely violated. Although feelings of guilt and self-blame are common following an incident of sexual abuse, such feelings impede recovery and must be addressed.

Is prostitution a form of sexual abuse?

While payment for sex may seem like an ethically neutral activity between consenting adults, prostitution and sexual abuse go hand in hand. Prostitutes are frequently raped by customers and pimps, were frequently raped and molested prior to becoming prostitutes, and are frequently coerced into continuing their "profession." In fact recent studies show that most prostitutes want to quit and that most have symptoms of PTSD.

Do victims of sexual abuse display any particular symptoms?

Symptoms reported immediately following an incident of sexual abuse include anxiety, decreased interest in sexual activities, sleeping problems, and physical symptoms including rashes, stomach problems, and vaginal infection. Feelings include guilt, self-blame, self-hatred, anger, and fear. In addition, society sometimes blames victims for bringing on the event themselves. Although this attitude is not as widespread today as in previous years, and legal systems are taking a much firmer hand against sexual abuse offenders, blaming victims for inciting sexual abuse continues to exist.

Long-term effects of rape and sexual abuse include a marked decrease in sexual activity, which when it occurs is often disturbed by flashbacks to the event, intrusive thoughts, fear, and depression.

Is it possible to prevent PTSD from occurring after an incident of rape or sexual abuse?

As with all incidents of trauma, immediate intervention following a traumatic incident can greatly reduce if not completely prevent long-term symptoms from occurring. However, it seems that many survivors of rape do not seek treatment immediately following the event. Instead, they tend to attempt to cope with their symptoms themselves. In an effort perhaps to prove that they were not lessened or defeated by the violent assault, they attempt to put the incident behind them and return to normal living as quickly as possible. Coping this way has proved helpful for many women, but for others this essential denial leads to the emergence of additional symptoms years down the road.

DOMESTIC ABUSE

What constitutes domestic abuse?

Domestic abuse is any form of deliberate cruelty in a domestic situation, including physical, sexual, emotional, and verbal abuse. Physically abusive situations, however, usually include all four types of abuse. Physical abuse in a domestic situation is known as battery. In order to establish a pattern of battery, at least two incidents of deliberate physical assault must have occurred. However, in spite of the legal definitions of battery, studies prove that psychological humiliation produced by verbal and emotional abuse is as damaging as physical aggression and that women tend to retain memories of their psychological abuse as vividly as those of battering.

What constitutes battery?

Battery consists of any action that is inflicted on another person with an intent to do bodily harm. In some states, even threats to do bodily harm are considered to be a form of battery and are therefore illegal.

Battery includes, hitting, kicking, slapping, biting, and shoving, as well as the use of weapons ranging from household objects to firearms.

Do women commit battery?

Yes, they do. Although most incidents of physical abuse are committed by men, recent studies are beginning to document a rise in physical abuse committed by women.

Why do people stay in abusive relationships?

This is a concept that is difficult for anyone who has never been a victim of domestic violence to understand. The impulse is to ask, "If things are so terrible, why don't you just get up and leave?" But leaving is difficult, however, and people stay in abusive relationships for many reasons. In some instances, abusers knowingly create situations where escape is virtually impossible. In extreme cases, victims are actually tied up or locked in a room. More often, though, abusers threaten their spouses with further battery or even death or threaten to hurt other family members or to harm family pets. In many cases, too, abusers control all the family finances, fostering a deep sense of dependency in their victims.

But more importantly, victims of domestic abuse develop such low self-esteem as a result of their experience that they lack any confidence to do anything on their own. It is true that some people remain in abusive relationships because they mistakenly believe their kids would be better off, and some remain because they want desperately to believe that the violence will never happen again, or because deep down they genuinely love the person, but in most cases the violence has rendered its victim dysfunctional, making escape almost impossible to accomplish.

Are there any recognizable factors that may contribute to domestic abuse?

Studies conducted primarily on men who have battered their wives reveal a typical profile of particular characteristics, the most stark being that the majority of these men were themselves victims of abuse as children.

Studies such as these point to the frightening conclusion that victims of childhood abuse grow up to become abusers themselves. Other characteristics observed include extreme jealousy, a fear of being abandoned, a poor frustration tolerance, a quick temper, poor problem-solving skills, poor interpersonal skills, and habitual alcohol or drug abuse.

Sociological factors that contribute to domestic violence include unemployment, poverty, and poor health.

Does domestic abuse only occur in low-income families?

No, this is a common misconception. Domestic abuse can and does occur at all levels of the economic strata.

Should I believe it when my partner assures me that the violence will never happen again?

You may want to believe your partner when you are told that the violence will never occur again, but you would most likely be kidding yourself. Although single incidents of violence do happen, for the most part incidents of domestic violence occur in recognizable cycles, over and over again.

My husband only hits me when he's drunk. Is this common?

Yes. Alcohol is a precipitating element in most incidents of domestic violence.

What sort of impact does domestic violence have on its victims?

The impact of domestic violence is extensive, including:

- physical injuries such as black eyes, broken bones and teeth, burns, and internal injuries

- psychological injuries such as feelings of fear, worthlessness, hopelessness, depression, anger, and grief
- alienation and social isolation
- a diminished capacity to problem-solve

Why do many cases of domestic abuse go unreported?

- Because of the humiliation involved, victims deny that they are being abused.
- Many victims genuinely (usually with good reason) fear the possibility of retaliation more than the abuse itself.
- Victims fear the unknown—they believe that their current situation is better than the prospects of facing life alone without any resources. Better the devil you know!
- Victims are afraid of becoming involved with law enforcement agencies. They are concerned that they may lose more, such as their children.

What can I do about my situation?

Shelters, hot lines, and community crisis centers are available to help victims of domestic violence. If you are being battered in your home, contact one of these resources (See the Resources section in the back of the book). Remember, battery is a serious crime and needs to be reported to your local precinct. The police department will also be able to advise you regarding "orders of protection" that can be obtained through the courts. Taking out an "order of protection" against someone means that you can have them arrested if they come near you.

WAR AND COMBAT

What is the impact of war on its veterans?

At least a quarter of combat veterans come home with
PTSD. Untreated, their complex of symptoms can torment them for decades. In addition, they frequently
suffer from depression and substance abuse.

**Why is there such a high incidence of alcohol and drug
abuse among war veterans?**

Alcohol and drugs are common forms of rest and recre-
ation among young soldiers in the field, serving not
only to relieve the fears and pain of physical combat,
but also to while away the hours of boredom spent
awaiting orders. Consistent use of addictive substances
inevitably leads to addictions that continue once the
veteran returns to civilian life. Drug and alcohol addictions also develop in veterans as they attempt to relieve
some of the painful symptoms of PTSD that develop
when they return to civilian life.

**Do all war veterans develop PTSD after serving their
time?**

No. In spite of the horrors of war, not all veterans go
on to develop PTSD, but the percentage of those who
do is very high. A study (the National Vietnam Veterans Readjustment Study) conducted in the late 1980s
found that 35.8 percent of those studied displayed
symptoms of full-blown PTSD, while over 70 percent
indicated that they had experienced at least some of the
symptoms during the twenty-year period following
combat.

In fact, most veterans do not escape unscathed.
Many suffer from physical disabilities or addictions
that make employment difficult or even impossible, or

have emotional problems that wreak havoc on interpersonal relationships, resulting in unusually high divorce rates. Clinical depression is also extremely
prevalent among combat veterans.

**I've heard that a large percentage of homeless people
are war veterans. Is this true?**

Unfortunately, yes. According to the National Coalition for the Homeless, on any given night, between
150,000 and 250,000 war veterans show up at shelters.

Can war cause PTSD in others besides combatants?

Yes. PTSD can affect anyone associated with the horrors of war, including medical personnel responsible
for treating the injured, office personnel charged with
documenting the dead, and innocent civilians.

**Are there any specific factors that contribute to the
high percentage of PTSD among combat victims?**

Yes. The relatively young age and emotional immatur-
ity of most soldiers is a huge contributing factor. The
normal stages of development that occur during late
adolescence and early adulthood are disrupted. This is
the time when career choices are being made, intimate
relationships based on mutual sharing and caring are
being formed, and people are learning how to integrate
their individual needs and desires with the social and
moral demands imposed by their society. The very nature of military life and combat disrupts this necessary
stage of emotional development. It demands physical
separation from loved ones, the relinquishment of
one's autonomy, and the enhancement of ideals and
practices that promote violence and killing. In addition, military training and combat itself involve actively learning to respond to feelings of anger with acts

of violence. Soldiers are also expected to subjugate the experience of all other emotions, such as fear, tenderness, and grief, in order to withstand the harshness of war. Many veterans returning home have great difficulty adjusting to civilian life, where actively experiencing a wide range of human emotions is normal and responding to anger with violence is unacceptable. The fact that the very skills which are needed for one's survival on the battlefield are those which are so contrary to survival in normal civilian life creates a paradox that has heartbreaking repercussions for returning veterans.

NATURAL DISASTERS

When the floods destroyed my home and the homes of my family, I knew it was because I had sinned.

The belief that everything happens for a reason is a common philosophy, particularly when natural disasters strike. It may be comforting to yield to the mercy of God or nature, but it can also be hurtful when one believes that the disaster itself had something to do with his or her personal behavior. You might find it useful to explore the logic in your thinking and the psychological reasons behind your guilt. You might also find it useful to discuss your concerns with a trusted religious leader.

Are there any particular symptoms found among victims of natural disasters?

In addition to the various stress-related reactions discussed in other parts of the book, certain peculiar behaviors have been noted in victims of natural disasters. It seems that some people, in an attempt perhaps to create some sense of order in their lives, engage in various ritualistic types of behavior or make active attempts to change certain aspects of their lifestyle.

CHILD ABUSE

What constitutes child abuse?

Child abuse refers to a pattern of battery, emotional abuse, neglect, or sexual abuse inflicted on a child (that is, a person under eighteen years of age) by a parent, relative, baby-sitter, or any other primary caregiver. According to the definition used by the National Center on Child Abuse and Neglect (NCCAN), physical abuse includes any action that leads to bodily harm. Emotional abuse refers to verbal abuse, confinement, or any other action knowingly designed to inflict psychological harm on the child. Neglect is not providing for the welfare of the child, including the failure to provide adequate food, clothing, medical treatment, or schooling. And sexual abuse refers to any form of sexual contact, including but not limited to incest, prostitution, and sexual molestation, including forcing a child to expose their genitals.

What are some of the symptoms associated with abused children?

In cases of physical abuse or neglect, the signs are usually fairly overt. The child presents with physical injuries, including bruises, burns, broken bones, and unusual markings. Frequent accidents may also be a sign. For this reason, emergency room personnel are specifically trained to investigate unusual injuries and frequent trips to the ER. With neglect, signs are also pretty clear. Children may appear dirty, unkempt, and undernourished or show signs of not receiving adequate medical care. Emotional and sexual abuse are less easy to detect. Because there are no real physical signs, symptoms may manifest in their behaviors, which on their own can reflect any of a number of other conditions. For example, children may present as overly passive or aggressive. They may be depressed and socially isolated, with few or even no friends. Or they may be unmotivated at school, with failing grades, poor concentration, or a tendency toward truancy. Although the above behaviors can be an indication that some form of abuse is occurring at home, abused children are frequently misdiagnosed as hyperactive, depressed, or suffering from one of many personality or psychiatric disorders.

Besides abuse in the home, are there other ways that children can be abused?

Yes, children can be and are physically or sexually abused by acquaintances and strangers all the time—the kind old man down the street who always gives out candy, a visiting friend of the family, a stranger asking for directions. Often the abusers are people you would least expect. Children are also abused by other children or by merciless pimps who lure innocent runaways into lives of prostitution, pornography, and sexual slavery. Child labor, a crime in the United States, is also considered to be a form of abuse.

What is the long-term impact of child abuse?

Without intervention, child abuse can lead to a lasting impairment of the child's physical and mental health, including the development of symptoms associated with PTSD. These symptoms continue into adult life, resulting in dysfunctional behaviors, intimacy problems, substance abuse, and clinical depression. As adults, victims may become involved in crime, and a large percentage will end up abusing their own children.

Can children develop PTSD?

Yes, anyone at any age can develop PTSD. As with adults, children can develop the symptoms of PTSD after being exposed to any situation that is life threatening or perceived to be life threatening. In fact, children stand a greater chance of developing PTSD than adults, because children have not had the time or the opportunity to develop a mature set of coping skills.

The traumatic experiences of children often involve abuse by parents or other caregivers (those who should be providing for their safety and nurturing), resulting in an ongoing sense of betrayal and fear and an overwhelming feeling of helplessness, placing them at high risk for developing PTSD.

Does PTSD manifest in children the same way as in adults?

Yes and no. Yes, in that in order to be diagnosed with PTSD, the child must show symptoms from all three categories set forth in the DSM-IV, but no in that the symptoms themselves manifest a little differently in children, and some symptoms that are common in adults are very rare indeed in children. Flashbacks and intrusive thinking are apparently uncommon in children, although the traumatic memory is relived or reenacted through daydreams, repetitive play, or terrible nightmares. Children, unlike adults, tend not to relive the experience as it actually happened, but are more likely to use games or symbols to represent their horrific experience. For example, children may engage in rough or aggressive play with their toys or with other children or experience nightmares where they are frightened not by the offender or the traumatic event, but by stereotypical symbols of fear such as monsters or bogeymen.

Emotional numbing and amnesia are also symptoms not commonly found among children, although children may deliberately refuse to talk or even think about the event. Other symptoms prevalent among children who suffer from PTSD include problems at school, high levels of anxiety, and a variety of relatively minor physical symptoms including headaches, stomachaches, and the like. More serious symptoms include losing touch with reality, multiple personality disorders, and suicidal thoughts. Sexually inappropriate behaviors, crime, and self-injurious behaviors such as eating disorders and substance abuse are also common.

I was abused as a child. As an adult, will I still bear the scars?

You probably will. Sadly, the losses suffered by an abused child tend to be long and far-reaching. Feelings of pain, fear, betrayal, and hopelessness can be created by the contradictory nature of their relationship with the abuser (sex disguised as love, beatings as discipline). This can lead to an inability to trust others and form healthy relationships. At the same time, many people who were abused as children have compensated in other ways and can make use of their strengths to become more whole.

Is there any help available for children who are being abused?

Yes. If you are an abused child or if you know of a child who is being abused, you can file a report with your local Office of Child Protective Services. Hot lines and toll-free numbers are also available to hook you up with organizations and people who will be able to help (see the Resources section in the back of book). If you were abused as a child but have not sought help, support groups for adults abused as children are also available.

How is PTSD treated in children?

The initial concern in treating PTSD is safety, and so it is important that the child is removed from the source of the trauma. While this sometimes means removal from a parent, treatment can usually be begun without such a drastic change.

With regard to therapy, play therapy tends to be the most effective for toddlers and younger children. By means of dolls, drawing materials, and other toys, therapists help children identify and work through their fears and anxieties. With older children and teenagers, individual supportive psychotherapy and behavior therapy as well as family therapy are useful. As with adults, some of the symptoms of PTSD can be controlled by the use of medication.

References

Flannery, R. B., *Post-Traumatic Stress Disorder: The Victim's Guide to Healing and Recovery*. New York: Crossroads Publishing, 1992.

Matsakis A. *I Can't Get Over It: A Handbook for Trauma Survivors*. Oakland, Calif.: New Harbinger Publications, 1996.

Matsakis, A. *Post-Traumatic Stress Disorder: A Complete Treatment Guide*. Oakland, Calif.: New Harbinger Publications, 1994.

Shay, J. "Shattered Lives." *The Family Therapy Networker*, July/August 1996, p. 46.

Chapter 10

RECOVERY AND EMPOWERMENT

How long will recovery take?

This is a difficult question to answer, because it depends on a whole group of variables. If it is a single incident of trauma, such as a natural disaster, prompt attention could minimize PTSD by nipping it in the bud. Some therapists who focus on using cognitive-behavioral or brief psychotherapeutic techniques believe that treatment of PTSD after such traumas could take days, weeks, or months. Often, however, treatment of chronic PTSD may be necessary for several months or even for years. Largely, though, much of the recovery process will depend on you and the effort you put into healing yourself. As emphasized throughout the book, just as your response to the trauma was unique to you and just as your treatment plan will be tailor-made to suit your specific needs, so too will the recovery process.

Will I be able to fully recover from my trauma?

This is also a difficult question to answer. Some people do experience a full recovery, while for others, recovery may mean learning to cope more effectively with their symptoms. It may be that once PTSD has taken hold, it could be too much to expect a prompt resolution of all symptoms and that the focus of therapy should be rather to prevent your symptoms from getting worse by teaching symptom management techniques, by improving your overall health, and by reestablishing your personal identity. However, do not feel demoralized by this answer. If you follow the suggestions set forward in this book in securing professional help and maintaining a positive and determined attitude toward getting well, you should find yourself feeling stronger and more content.

How will I know that I have recovered?

As you work through your issues and develop ways to calm and soothe yourself, you may notice periods of calm. You may notice increased pleasure. You may feel greater enthusiasm and trust. You may forget about your trauma for prolonged periods of time. No one feels good all the time, but resolution of PTSD means a greater sense of well-being.

I'm afraid of change. Will I be the same person as I was before the trauma occurred?

Fear is a central component of PTSD. Fear drives most of the crippling symptoms of PTSD. One of the difficult aspects in PTSD treatment is that even confronting the illness can be enormously frightening. As you work through your PTSD, you may indeed find that the treatment has changed you. Much of that change may include a greater control over your fear and a greater sense of control over your life. You may be stronger than you were before the trauma, and, in that way, you may be different.

What is meant by "empowerment"?

Empowerment means being able to gain a sense of control over your life. Not just doing what you want, but also being able to soothe and relax yourself on command. This is a very difficult skill for people with PTSD, often because relaxation and calm feel intensely threatening to people with PTSD. These skills may be difficult, but they're vital to your recovery. Remember, when you were traumatized, you were essentially robbed of your sense of having control over your life—you were probably rendered helpless and powerless. Becoming empowered is when you regain those feelings of being in control and have the strength and the courage to move forward with your life.

What if I don't get better?

Many people with PTSD don't improve for years at a time. Some seem to just get worse. That is one of the main reasons for this book. Try different approaches. If you've tried one type of treatment, try another. Try meditation. If meditation makes you nervous or bored, try a variant of meditation. For example, practice looking at a candle for a few moments and noticing what you feel. Record that feeling in a notebook, blow out the candle, and try again the next day. The goal of all treatments should be to try to help you feel better. Your job is to keep making use of the various possibilities and make them work for you.

My life is stressful and difficult right now, but at least I am familiar with it. I'm concerned that if I go for treatment and start opening up, I may lose control.

That's exactly the concern of so many people with PTSD. People with PTSD often fear that they'll lose control of something: their rage, their sense of themselves, their ability to physically move. Safety might be the most important issue when it comes to PTSD, which is one reason why an ongoing relationship with a therapist can be a useful way to contain this sense of loss of control. If you get to know a therapist and develop a sense of trust, you might learn that you can lose control a little without a calamity occurring.

You keep saying that making my own choices and decisions about my treatment will help with my recovery, but I feel like I can't think for myself anymore.

Be aware that people with PTSD tend to be very critical of themselves and also tend to globally dismiss their own competence. Try to recognize the gradual improvements that you've made and be aware that you are almost always capable of making significant decisions for yourself.

Can PTSD be prevented?

Studies suggest that early intervention (immediately following the traumatic event) can significantly reduce the chances of developing PTSD. This would include eliciting support from your family and from your community, making use of many of the emergency services and specific organizations that are available to help victims, and learning as much as possible about the nature of PTSD.

What are emergency services?

Emergency services are state or government services that automatically go into effect after a disaster occurs. They are the services that provide food, shelter, medical treatment, counseling, and other amenities that victims may need to begin to put their lives back together. Some services go into effect when a person is admitted into an emergency room (social work services, psychiatric services, victims' assistance programs, etc.), and some services are mobilized out in the field when natural disasters (such as hurricanes and floods) or manmade disasters (such as bombings and terrorist attacks). It is in your best self-interest to utilize as many of these services as you can. Remember, these people are skilled professionals experienced in dealing with trauma.

What is Critical Stress Debriefing (CSD)?

CSD is a form of crisis intervention. It is an emergency service utilized in situations where many people are affected by one disaster, for example, when a hurricane destroys a town or a building is bombed by terrorists. It is a brief powerful technique, whereby victims are brought together as a group to promote a sense of solidarity and shared suffering, and to provide suggestions as to what people should expect over the next few days. It also offers specific coping techniques. One by one, people are asked to describe the event and to share their experience with the group—how they felt and how they were affected. By describing their own experiences and by listening to the experiences of others, victims learn that what they are feeling is normal, and they develop a sense of solidarity with the group. They realize that they are all in it together. CSD is also useful for emergency personnel who may become traumatized in the line of duty. CSD is a powerful form of crisis intervention and has proved successful in preventing the development of PTSD in many victims.

Can the judicial system be of help?

For victims of certain types of trauma such as rape, robbery, or assault, or in situations where the trauma was caused by the negligence of another party or organization, the police department, the courts, and victim assistance programs can provide help in securing compensation for their loss. If you consider taking this route, however, you need to think it over carefully, because legal recourse can also be harmful in that it frequently results in retraumatization. For example, you may have to testify in court or be subjected to hours of painful interrogation about the event. If, however, seeking help through the judicial system will bring a sense of closure or help to lessen your feelings of injustice, this system should be utilized.

Will I really be able to put all this behind me and move on with my life?

In some fashion, we all have to put the stresses and minor traumas of our lives behind us. People with PTSD do have a bigger mountain to climb. Keep at it. The diagnosis of PTSD has been widely recognized for only a short period of time. Treatments are constantly being refined. Therapists are becoming more expert every day. As are you. Good luck.

Resources:

SUPPORT GROUPS AND
REFERRAL SYSTEMS

Alcoholism
AA World Service (Alcoholics Anonymous)
P.O. Box 459, Grand Central Station
New York, NY 10163
(212) 870–3400

Al-Anon Family Group Headquarters and Alateen
(for families of alcoholics)
World Service Office
P.O. Box 862, Midtown Station
New York, NY 10018
(212) 737–8524

Child Abuse
Incest Survivors Anonymous
P.O. Box 17245
Long Beach, CA 90807
(310) 428–5599

National Center for Child Abuse and Neglect
107 Lincoln Street
Huntsville, AL 35801
(205) 534–6868

National Council on Child Abuse and Female Violence
1155 Connecticut Avenue NW, Suite 400
Washington, DC 20036
(800) 222–2000

VOICES in Action *(incest survivors' network)*
P.O. Box 148309
Chicago, IL 60614
(312) 327–1500

Domestic Violence
National Coalition Against Domestic Violence
P.O. Box 18749
Denver, CO 80218
(303) 839–1852

National Council on Child Abuse and Female Violence
1155 Connecticut Avenue, NW, Suite 400
Washington, DC 20036
(800) 222–2000

Victim Services
2 Lafayette Street
New York, NY 10007
212–577–7700
www.dvsheltertour.org

Mental Health
Anxiety Disorders Association of America
6000 Executive Boulevard
Rockville, MD 20852–3801
(301) 831–8350

International Society for Traumatic Stress Studies
60 Revere Drive, Suite 500
Northbrook, IL 60062
(708) 480–9080

National Alliance for the Mentally Ill
200 North Glede Road, Suite 1015
Arlington, VA 22203–3754
(703) 525–7600

National Center for Post-traumatic Stress Disorder
VAM & ROC 116D
Rural Route 5
White River Junction, VT 05009
(802) 296–5132

National Institute of Mental Health
Division of Communications
5600 Fishers Lane
Rockville, Maryland 20857
(301) 443–2403

National Mental Health Association
1021 Prince Street
Alexandria, VA 22314–2971
(703) 684–7722

Mourning:
Griefnet
www.griefnet.org

Rape and Abuse:
Rape Abuse and Incest National Network (RAINN)
800–656–HOPE (4673).
www.rainn.org

National Crime Victims Research and Treatment
center
Medical University of South Carolina
165 Cannon Street, P.O. Box 250852
Charleston, SC 29425
(843) 792–2945
www.musc.edu/cvc/

Specialized Therapies
EMDR—HAP (Eye Movement Densensitization and
Reprocessing—Humanitarian Assistance Program)
P.O. Box 1542
El Grenada, CA 94018
(415) 728–5609

EMDRIA (Eye Movement Desensitization and
Reprocessing International Association)
P.O. Box 140824
Austin, TX 78714–0824
(512) 451–0329
www.emdria.org

EMDR Institute (Eye Movement Desensitization and
Reprocessing Institute)
P.O. Box 51010
Pacific Grove, CA 93950–6010
(408) 372–3900

TFT: Thought Field Therapy *(Help for Anxiety,
Trauma, Grief, and Anger)*
(800) 656–4496

TIRA *(for information on Traumatic Incident Reduction Therapy)*
13 NW Barry Road, Suite 214
Kansas City, MO 64155–2728

(800) 499–2751
(816) 468–4945

Suicide
American Suicide Foundation
1045 Park Avenue
New York, NY 10028
(800) 531–4477

Ray-Of-Hope *(for suicide survivors)*
P.O. Box 2323
Iowa City, IA 52244
(319) 377–9890

Veterans
American Legion
1608 K Street NW
Washington, DC 20006
(202) 861–2700

Blinded Veterans Association
477 H Street NW
Washington, DC 20001
(202) 371–8880

Disabled American Veterans
807 Maine Avenue SW
Washington, DC 20024
(202) 554–3501

Jewish War Veterans
1811 R Street NW
Washington, DC 20009
(202) 265–6280

Paralyzed Veterans of America
801 18th Street NW
Washington DC 20006
(202) 872–1300

U.S. Veterans Administration Readjustment Counseling Service (10B/RC)
810 Vermont Avenue NW
Washington, DC 20410
(202) 233–3317

Veterans of the Vietnam War—National Headquarters
760 Jumper Road
Wilkes-Barre, PA 18702
(717) 825–7215

Vietnam Veterans of America
1224 M Street NW
Washington, DC 20005
(202) 628–2700 *(to locate a local chapter)*

Victim Assistance
National Organization for Victims' Assistance (NOVA)
1757 Park Road NW
Washington, DC 20010
(202) 232–6682

HOTLINES

Federal Emergency Management Agency (FEMA) *(for victims of disasters)*
(800) 462–9029

National Child Abuse Hotline
(800) 4-A-CHILD

National Domestic Violence Hotline
(800) 779-7233

AIDS
National AIDS Hotline
(English)800-342-AIDS (Open 24 hrs.)
(Spanish)800-344-7432 (Open 8am-2am)
(TTY/TDD)800-243-7889(M-F 10am-10pm)

Alcohol and Drug Abuse
Alcohol and Drug Abuse Hotline
800-237-6237

Alcoholics Anonymous
212-870-3400
(or look for a local number in any telephone book)

Narcotics Anonymous
(818) 773-9999

Anxiety and Panic
National Institute of Mental Health Panic Campaign
800-64-PANIC

Child Abuse and Domestic Violence
Child Abuse Hotline
800-792-5200

National Domestic Violence/Abuse Hotline
800-799-SAFE
(TDD) 800-787-3224

VOICES
Victims of Incest Can Emerge Survivors
800–7–VOICE–8

Children and Teens
Boys Town National Hotline
800–448–3000
(TDD) 800–448–1833

Covenant House Nineline
800–999–9999

National Center for Missing and Exploited Children
800–843–5678
(TDD)800–826–7653

National Runaway Hotline
800–231–6946

National Youth Crisis Hotline
800–442–HOPE

Depression
Depression Awareness
800–421–4211

Rape and Sexual Assault
RAINN
Rape, Abuse, Incest National Network
800–656–HOPE

Victims of Crime Resources Center
800–842–8467

Suicide Prevention and Crisis Intervention
Crisis Intervention Center
800–333–4444

Help Now Hotline
800–435–7609

National Adolescent Suicide Hotline
800–621–4000

Glossary

Abuse: To physically or verbally attack or injure.

Acupuncture: An ancient form of Chinese medicine that attempts to cure pain or illness by stimulating specific points of the body thought to be associated with the flow of bio-energy. Small sharp needles are used.

Acute Symptoms: Symptoms that begin suddenly with a marked intensity and then subside after a relatively short period of time.

Adrenaline: A hormone produced primarily by the adrenal gland in order to increase overall metabolism and prepare the body for action against a perceived threat.

Alcoholism: A condition or disease caused by an addiction to alcoholic beverages.

Amnesia: Memory loss caused by a head injury or by psychological trauma.

Analgesics: Painkillers.

Anger Management: A structured technique involving relaxation methods used to control intense reactions to rage.

Antidepressants: Medications used to treat depression.

Antipsychotics: Medications used to treat conditions of psychosis (such as schizophrenia) and other psychotic reactions. (They may also be useful for symptoms of PTSD.)

Anxiety: An unpleasant state of tension and uneasiness not usually associated with any specific stimulants.

Anxiety Disorders: Psychiatric diseases, marked by a heightened state of fear.

Arouse: To evoke action or response to sensory stimuli.

Avoidance: A conscious or unconscious defense mechanism by which an individual tries to avoid escape from unpleasant stimuli, conflicts, or feelings (such as anxiety, fear, or pain).

Behavior Therapy: A form of psychotherapy that attempts to modify observable maladjusted patterns of behavior by substituting a new response or set of responses to a given stimuli.

Biofeedback: A method of learning to control one's bodily or mental functions using the aid of a visual or auditory display of one's own brain waves, blood pressure, etc.

Brief Psychotherapy: Any psychotherapeutic modality that focuses on a specific goal and is concluded after several weeks to one year.

Chronic Condition: A condition or disease that develops slowly and occurs for a long period of time or frequently reoccurs.

Cognitive Therapy: A form of therapy that attempts to change attitudes, perceptions, and patterns of thinking.

Denial: An unconscious defense mechanism whereby emotional conflict and anxiety are avoided by refusing to acknowledge those thoughts, feelings, desires, impulses, or external facts that are unconsciously intolerable.

Depression: A severe state of sadness, hopelessness, pessimism, and uselessness that leads to an impairment in daily functioning.

Dopamine: One of the brain chemicals thought to play a role in controlling mood.

EMDR: Eye Movement Desensitization and Reprocessing. This is a form of therapy that combines aspects of a number of different treatment techniques with specific eye movements.

Endorphins: Chemicals that are produced by the brain

and that closely resemble the opiates found in drugs such as morphine.

Flashbacks: The sudden reexperiencing of traumatic events as though they are reoccurring, usually in response to an environmental trigger of some kind.

Flooding: A behavior-therapy technique used to treat phobias and anxiety by submitting the person to large doses of the feared stimulus.

Grief: Periods of normal sadness or melancholia following the death of a loved one.

Group Therapy: The application of psychotherapy within a small group of people who all experience similar difficulties.

Gynecologist: A doctor who specializes in treating conditions of the reproductive organs of women.

Homicide: The killing of one human being by another.

Hormone: A chemical substance produced by one organ which regulates the functioning of another.

Hyperarousal: The state of increased physical arousal that includes symptoms such as insomnia, irritability, and being easily startled.

Hypervigilance: The state of being overprotective about one's safety or the safety of others by always being on the alert for danger.

Hypnosis: An artificially induced sleeplike state of altered awareness.

Hypnotherapy: A form of therapy that uses hypnosis to place a client into a state of relaxed wakefulness and heightened concentration, usually used for retrieving repressed memories.

Incest: Sexual relations between members of the same family who are so closely related that marriage is legally forbidden.

Insomnia: An inability to sleep.

Internist: A physician who specializes in internal medicine.

Interpersonal Psychotherapy: A form of psychotherapy that focuses on conflicts and difficulties that people have in their relationships with others.

Limbic System: A group of structures found in the brain that are associated with various emotions and feelings such as anger, fear, sexual arousal, pleasure, and sadness.

Meditation: A stress reduction technique that focuses on breath, a word, or an action to balance physical, mental, and emotional states.

Monoamine Oxidase Inhibitors (MAOI's): Antidepressant medications that inhibit an enzyme that breaks down noradrenaline, making it available to the brain.

Mood Stabilizers: Drugs that are used to block both manic and depressive symptoms at the same time, for example, lithium.

Neuropeptide: A chemical that facilitates communication between brain cells.

Paranoia: A disorder characterized by overly suspicious thinking that may include delusions of persecution or grandeur.

Psychiatry: The study of diseases and disorders of the mind.

Psychoanalysis: An approach to psychotherapy attributed to Sigmund Freud which is based on the concept that human behavior and emotions are directed by unconscious thoughts, wishes, and feelings.

Psychodynamic Psychotherapy: A form of talk therapy that focuses on the forces that moderate behavior, specifically the influence of past experiences on present behavior.

Psychopharmacology: The use of medication to treat psychiatric disorders.

Psychosomatic Condition: The expression of an emotional conflict through physical symptoms.

Psychotherapist: A trained professional who uses psychological methods to help people overcome or cope with mental illness.

Repression: An unconscious defense mechanism whereby unacceptable thoughts, feelings, ideas, impulses, or memories (especially those concerning some traumatic event) are pushed out of conscious awareness because of their painful content.

Selective Serotonin Reuptake Inhibitors (SSRI's): Antidepressant medications that increase the availability of serotonin to the brain.

Serotonin: A brain chemical thought to control mood and states of consciousness.

Shell Shock: A name coined during World War I for the PTSD symptoms suffered by soldiers as a result of combat.

Stressor: Anything that causes wear or tear on one's physical or mental resources.

Supportive Psychotherapy: A talk therapy that focuses on the here and now. The therapist is active in providing guidance, advice, and direction.

Systematic Desensitization: A technique used in behavior therapy for eliminating maladaptive anxiety associated with phobias.

TFT: Thought Field Therapy. A newly developed therapy for treating trauma based on the philosophy of Chinese acupuncture.

TIR: Traumatic Incident Reduction. A brief therapy used for treating trauma based on the principles of systematic desensitization.

Traumatic Bonding: An alliance that develops between captives and their captors whereby the captives internalize the philosophies of their captors.

Tricyclic Antidepressants (TCA's): Medications used to treat depression so named because of their three-ringed chemical structure.

VKD: Visual Kinesthetic Dissociation. A new form of psychodynamic therapy used specifically to treat victims of trauma whereby victims are required to step outside of their experience and look at it as though they are watching a movie.

Selected Readings

BOOKS

Bisby, Stephen, and Lori Beth Bisby. *Brief Therapy for Post-Traumatic Stress Disorder, Traumatic Incident Reduction and Related Techniques*. New York: John Wiley & Sons, 1998.

Brown, Daniel. *Art Therapies*. London: Thorsons (an imprint of HarperCollins Publishers), 1997.

Coffey, Rebecca. *Unspeakable Truths and Happy Endings*. Lutherville, Md.: Sidran Press, 1998.

Davidson, Johnathan R. T., and Edna B. Foa, Ph.D., eds. *Post-Traumatic Stress Disorder, DSM-IV and Beyond*. Washington, DC: American Psychiatric Association Press, 1993.

Herman, Judith, M.D. *Trauma and Recovery*. New York: Basic Books, 1997.

Levine, Peter A. *Waking the Tiger: Healing Trauma*. Berkeley, CA: North Atlantic Books, 1996.

Matsakis, Aphrodite, Ph.D. *I Can't Get Over It: A Handbook for Trauma Survivors*. 2nd edition. Oakland, Calif.: New Harbinger Publications, 1996.

Matsakis, Aphrodite, Ph.D. *Post-Traumatic Stress Disorder: A Complete Treatment Guide*. Oakland Calif.: New Harbinger Publications, 1994.

Parnell, Laurel, Ph.D. *Transforming Trauma: EMDR*. New York: Norton, 1998.

Winn, Linda. *Post-Traumatic Stress Disorder and Dramatherapy: Treatment and Risk Reduction*. London: Jessica Kingsley Publishers, 1994.

Index